Why I Left the Amish

Why I Left the Amish

a memoir by SALOMA MILLER FURLONG

MICHIGAN STATE UNIVERSITY PRESS | *East Lansing*

Copyright © 2011 by Saloma Miller Furlong

 The paper used in this publication meets the minimum requirements
of ANSI/NISO Z39.48-1992 (R 1997) (Permanence of Paper).

Michigan State University Press
East Lansing, Michigan 48823-5245

Printed and bound in the United States of America.

17 16 15 14 13 12 11   1 2 3 4 5 6 7 8 9 10

LIBRARY OF CONGRESS CATALOGING-IN-PUBLICATION DATA
Furlong, Saloma Miller.
Why I left the Amish : a memoir / by Saloma Miller Furlong.
p. cm.
ISBN 978-0-87013-994-9 (pbk. : alk. paper) 1. Furlong, Saloma Miller. 2. Furlong, Saloma Miller—
Childhood and youth. 3. Furlong, Saloma Miller—Family. 4. Amish—Ohio—Biography.
5. Amish—Ohio—Social life and customs. 6. Parent and child—Ohio. 7. Families—Ohio. I. Title.
F500.M45F87 2011
977.1'044—dc22
2010042292

Book and cover design by Charlie Sharp, Sharp Des!gns, Lansing, Michigan

Michigan State University Press is a member of the Green Press Initiative and is committed to developing and
encouraging ecologically responsible publishing practices. For more information about the Green Press Initiative
and the use of recycled paper in book publishing, please visit *www.greenpressinitiative.org*.

Visit Michigan State University Press on the World Wide Web at *www.msupress.msu.edu*

For David who has inscribed love on my heart,
where it shall remain forever

To Paul and Tim who inherit the family stories

In memory of Datt, Mem, and Lizzie

Contents

Acknowledgments

*M*y deepest gratitude is owed to David who helped me keep the faith that my story would eventually find its way into print, and for his unending support through the many drafts and rejection letters. Much appreciation also goes to Julie Loehr, for her enthusiasm for and dedication to publishing this book; to all the rest of the team at Michigan State University Press for their expertise and sense of humor while shepherding the book to publication; to Jeanne Braham who helped me to shape my story into what it is; to Ilan Stavans, Valerie Hurley, Ute Brandes, Lucinda Martin, Janel Gamm, Francine Munson, Carol McQuillen, Deborah and Sarah Elkinton, and others who read my story at least once during its evolution and who gave me encouragement and valuable feedback; and to Kari Jo Spear and members of writing critique groups who helped me develop my writing style and voice. To the many friends in Vermont and elsewhere who have been waiting for years to read my story—this book is for you.

My story could never have been written (indeed my life could not have been lived in the manner in which it has) without embarking on a healing journey first. I will be forever grateful to Rachel Harrer, Brookes Cowan, Melita DeBellis, and Tyler Gould for lending me a hand along the way, and for helping me to live the life I have chosen.

And last but not least, I will be forever grateful to Smith College and its many excellent professors for providing me with a *Bildung*—an education that not only developed my knowledge, but also helped build my character. A special thanks goes to Ellie Rothman for establishing the Ada Comstock Scholars Program, which provided me with the sense of being in the right place, doing the right thing, at the right time.

Why I Left the Amish

Datt's Struggle with Life

There are two ways to leave the Amish—one is through life and the other through death. To leave through life, someone has to deliberately walk away from the security and conformity of the strictly ordered community. Once abandoned, the future is self-determined, exhilarating, and terrifyingly open. Anyone who lives the life determined by the community leaves solely through death.

My father (Datt) once tried doing it through life. He left the community, but like the prodigal son, he returned, and was forever remorseful and shamed for leaving the fold. There is a whole decade of his life I know very little about—only that he had left the Amish, joined the military during World War II, was honorably discharged shortly thereafter, and that he worked on the Baltimore and Ohio Railroad for some years. It seemed like he had tried to erase the experiences from this period of his life from his otherwise sharp memory by not talking about them at all. Asking him questions about this era was strictly forbidden. Now, in 2004, Datt was about to take his final leave of the Amish—this time through death.

My sister Susan had let me know that Datt had gone into the hospital with a collapsed lung. He had been fighting for every breath for the last three years with a chronic disease called Farmer's Lung, which was caused by being around moldy hay most of his life. There was no treatment for his stage of the illness. The health professionals had sent him home from the hospital after determining that there was nothing they could do to help him. I thought about traveling back to Ohio, but the timing of his illness made this a difficult decision. I had been craving more education ever since I was thirteen and had to leave school because it was "the Amish way." After I left the Amish, I got married and had children. I decided to wait until our two sons were grown to follow my dreams. My time had finally come when I was accepted into the Ada Comstock Program at Smith College, designed for women who had not finished college at the traditional age. My first few weeks at Smith were even better than I had imagined. My classes—beginning German, Scandinavian mythology, astronomy, and ethics—provided just the right mix to challenge and expand my thinking. If ever I was in the right place doing the right thing at the right time, this was it.

The moon lit up the autumn night as I drove through the mountains on my way to Smith College from my home in Vermont. I was talking to Datt as if he could hear me, although he was 550 miles away. "Datt, I hope you can go in peace, when it's your time to go. You've had a life filled with sorrow, so I hope you will find peace in dying and in the life beyond." I wiped the tears from my cheeks as I rounded the bend. Awestruck, I saw the moon suspended above the break in the trees, perfectly centered between two mountains where Route 103 cuts through the valley. It lit up the little town of Ludlow in the valley below. The symmetry and the beauty of the moment seemed to me a visual affirmation of my prayer. As if the moon was lighting my way, I realized that I needed to let Datt know my thoughts. I would write to him as a way of saying farewell.

When I arrived at 54 Green Street in Northampton, I carried my clean laundry and backpack of homework to my room, made my bed with fresh sheets, hung up my clothes, and then sat down at my desk and typed a letter to Datt. The words spilled out onto the page without effort as my tears dripped onto the keyboard.

September 19, 2004

Dear Datt,

I heard that you have been in the hospital and that you are now at home. I think it's great that you can be at home with Mem right now.

I think of you many times a day, and I find myself talking to you, as if you could hear me. I decided to let you know by letter, so that you really can hear me, as read to you by Mem.

I hope you can forgive me for the grief I caused you as I was growing up. I know I wasn't the easiest child to raise. I am also sorry for the guilt that you and Mem have shouldered all these years for the choices that I, as your grown daughter, made in leaving the Amish. I made the best choice for me, and I don't feel you and Mem should feel guilty for that. I am sorry that you have been made to feel that way, for that is a burden you and Mem shouldn't have to carry. I hope you have put that burden down, for I can (and should) own all the benefits and consequences for my decision. You have had more than your share of sorrows, without having that heaped on you, too.

Tonight I am recalling several fond memories from my childhood. Do you remember when you used to play the hand-stacking game with us when we were little? Your hand on the table, then mine, and your other hand, then my other hand, and we would take the bottom one out of the pile and slap it on the top of the pile over and over? Sometimes you would play it with two of us at a time. You used to play it after supper some nights.

One spring, during sugaring season, I helped gather nine tanks of sap. That night I brought you supper in the sugarhouse. I remember you saying, "Lomie, you did a good job gathering sap today. Thank you for your help." I knew you really meant it, because you didn't often say such things. It meant a lot to me that you said it.

Another time, when I was in my young teens, I had a hard time sleeping at night. I used to lie in my bed and cry. That went on for a long time. Then, one night you opened up the door at the bottom of the stairs and called up, "Lomie, you need to stop crying now and go to sleep." Your voice didn't have any anger in it, only kindness and understanding. I don't know why, but I was able to stop crying and I fell asleep. I don't remember having a problem sleeping after that night.

I am with you in spirit, as I think of you many times a day. I pray that you will soon be reunited with your father and other loved ones.

May you receive that love with open arms. Go in peace when your journey here on earth is at an end. And may we meet again someday.
　　Love from your daughter,
　　Saloma

I typed another letter to Mem and told her Datt's dying reminded me of the time my mother-in-law, Ruth, lay dying in Vermont. My husband, David, and I did not get a chance to say good-bye to her. I hoped Mem would read my letter to Datt. I didn't know how much of it he could comprehend, but I knew this was as much for me as for him.

Dear Mem,
　　I've been waiting to get news of Datt, so I can write to you, knowing at least a little of what is going on. I talked with Susie tonight who had the news through Lizzie. I understand that Datt is home from the hospital, and that he is on morphine to relieve his coughing. I also heard that he is able to talk and is aware of what is going on around him, but falls asleep often. It sounds to me as if he is about as comfortable as he can be in these circumstances.
　　I know that I asked you a little while ago what you need from me, and you said, "Write to me." I haven't been very good about that, and I'm sorry. My thoughts are with you a lot more often than my letters.
　　Is there anything I can do for you at this time? If you or Datt feel that you want me to travel to Ohio, please let me know. I am in my first couple weeks of classes, so this is a hard time for me to travel the distance, but I will if you and/or Datt would like me to.
　　Susie asked me tonight whether I am okay with the fact that I have probably seen Datt for the last time, and I said I am. I feel over the last ten years or so, that I have let go of hard feelings I had for anything that happened between him and me when I was young and still living at home. However, I decided to write a good-bye letter to Datt, and I am wondering if you would kindly read it to him? That is the one regret I had after David's mother died, is that I hadn't gotten a chance to say a proper good-bye to her. I think she would have liked to have that chance, too.
　　The way I am hearing you are accepting this, and the strength

you are exhibiting is wonderful. I believe that the Amish attitude about death and dying is so much healthier than that in mainstream America. I don't feel you cling to the people who are dying, but accept it as God's plan, and part of life. This is so different from what I experienced in David's family when Ruth was dying. Bob clung to her with everything he had.

I send prayers up for you every day. I hope you are granted the strength and grace to see Datt through this. I know that you will miss him, despite (and perhaps even because of) all the difficulties you have been through. May the unconditional love you have shown him all these years come back to you in ways you may never have expected.

Speaking of love, I send you mine. This letter is small, but it comes with oceans of feelings. Thank you in advance for reading the enclosed letter to Datt for me.

Love,

Saloma

After printing out the letters, I sat with my head in my hands, and I could see Datt lying in the narrow bed in the bleak bedroom in the Dodde (Grandfather) house he and Mem lived in. I could see him lying on his back, his bald head depressing the pillow. When I was a teenager, I used to be embarrassed by Datt's looks. His big head was misshapen—pointed at the top and astonishingly flat in the back. His Amish beard was untidy and seemed to be all the hair his head could manage. Datt had big dark-brown eyes that turned black and snapped open and shut when he was angry. He had a long hawk nose, a feature shared by his family. And then there was always Datt's sunken mouth, which came from his having no teeth. He had had no teeth for as long as I can remember, because Mem had convinced him that he would not be able to adjust to dentures. Putting all these features together, Datt didn't look like any other Amish father I knew. At the age when most young people want to be the same as others, Datt's distinct looks were a source of embarrassment I could have done without. In my Amish community, one's family is much of one's identity, and I could not distance myself from him. He was my father, and I could not trade him in for another, much as I wanted to. Not only was I embarrassed by him when I was growing up, I was also afraid of him.

I FIRST REALIZED that there was something wrong with Datt early in my childhood. On winter nights lit by a hissing gas lantern, Datt would sit in his rocking chair and talk with someone only he could see. Datt refused to leave his hickory rocker despite Mem's urging. The bitterest arguments between Mem and Datt happened on those dark winter nights in Ohio. My eyes would follow the shadows of my parents cast by the light of the lantern as they exchanged bitter words. I remember feeling paralyzed with fear, confusion, and helplessness. I wished Datt would just go and do the farm chores so that Mem's bickering would stop, but it seemed as though he couldn't—it was as if someone had strapped him to the rocking chair. Mem would shriek out her frustration: "I just can't do it all! I should not have to do your work and mine too!"

"I have done my share and I do work hard!" Datt would say, the words coming out in a muffled garble as though his tongue were tripping over itself in his toothless mouth.

"You work hard from your rocking chair? What about me? I work all the time. I carry the water and the wood, make meals, do the wash by hand, take care of the children, and keep the house clean—and that's not enough! Now you want me to go feed the chickens, the pigs, the horses, and the cow; do the milking and gather the eggs; and then come in and make supper too, while you sit there on the rocking chair? Why should I?"

"You were the one who wanted to have children. Now you have them!" Datt would say this with his arms folded across his chest and his shadow frantically rocking on the wall behind him.

Defeated, Mem would take down her old black coat from the hook by the cookstove in the corner of the kitchen, wriggle it on over her wide body, put on her old scarf, and leave, taking with her the only gas lantern we had. Mem spoke with her whole body when she was angry—normally she did not have a heavy footfall for someone her size, but when she was angry, she stomped so that I could feel each of her steps in the vibration of the floor. I can still hear her say the sharp words as she slammed the kitchen door: *"Hock uf dei Stuhl und läss mich oll die eiwet du dann!"* (Sit on your rocking chair and let me do all the work then!). We would be left in the dim and flickering light of the oil lamp. Datt would stop rocking and look at the kitchen door, then slowly start rocking again, with his feet crossed, back and forth over the hand-woven rug. I would be so hungry my stomach hurt, but I knew we couldn't eat until Mem was done with the chores and could make supper.

"Sarah, come here," Datt would say in his sorrowful voice. When she came and stood before him, he would pick her up and sit her on his lap, then rock back and forth, the bent hickory rocking chair creaking in the same place with each rock.

The sharp sound of Mem's angry words still hung in the room, as Datt and the rocking chair cast a big shadow on the wall that moved back and forth as he rocked. He would stop in the forward position, with his beard moving up and down and his dark eyes snapping. He seemed to be talking with someone. I would look up toward the ceiling, where he would be directing his angry whispers and gestures, and not see anyone. Then he would resume his rocking with his feet crossed, back and forth over the hand-woven rug, with his eerie shadow moving back and forth on the wall.

On one such night, I was holding onto the arm of the rocking chair and asking Sarah if she wanted to come and play dolls with me, when I got too close and Datt rocked on my big toe. The crunching sound came first, just before the crushing pain. I shrieked from the shock of it. I sat on the floor and cried and screamed so hard I couldn't catch my breath. I wondered if the rocker had cut off my toe, the pain was so terrific. I wanted Mem to come in. Datt tried to distract me by getting his metal matchbox from his pocket. I usually loved watching him unscrew the matchbox, then tilt the top to show the blue tips of the matches inside, but my toe hurt too much to pay any attention. Then he offered me a penny if I would stop crying. I tried, but my desire for the penny could not compare with the crushing pain in my toe, and I kept on screaming. Then Datt turned away from me and started rocking Sarah on his lap. When I realized that Datt was not going to help me or even go call Mem, my sobs came heaving out of my chest, not only from the pain, but also from the fear of recognizing that Datt could not help me, no matter what happened.

When Mem finally came in, I showed her my toe. Blood oozed from under my toenail, and my toe looked flat. I was still sniffling after my sobbing. My toe still hurt, but more like someone was pounding it with a hammer than the feeling that the toe had been broken off. She gave me water in a wash basin to soak my toe while she scolded Datt with her sharp voice: "You can't even take care of the children while I am outside doing *your* chores!" He sat with his arms folded across his chest, and he kept his lips pressed together so hard, it looked as though he had no mouth. Mem kept scolding: "You could have gotten her cold water to soak her toe!" Still Datt sat there and said nothing.

Mem stomped around the kitchen making supper. When she finally put the vegetable soup on the table and said, "Supper," I didn't complain. I didn't like vegetable soup, but I was hungry enough to eat almost anything. I had dried off my toe and put my black stocking back on.

Datt got up from the rocking chair and moved to the table. He waited until we were all gathered around the table and then said, *"Händt nunna"* (Hands down). Before and after every meal, we would all put our hands in our laps and bow our heads for a silent prayer. Datt would signal the end of the silence by sliding his hands off his lap and picking up his water glass. Mem reached to dip the soup into our bowls. Usually she served Datt first, but this time she set her jaw and took our bowls one at a time, starting with the youngest—Baby Susie's, then Sarah's, mine, Lizzie's, and Joey's. When we were crushing crackers into our soup and blowing on each spoonful to cool it, Mem finally served Datt, then herself. Then quiet set in, the kind that made me afraid of what would happen next. The fear that lived inside the quiet was like a bottomless black pit. Sometimes, when I went to bed at night, I would feel that blackness inside of me. Then one night the blackness took the form of a horrible nightmare.

The dream started out much like real life, with Datt sitting on his rocking chair. He sat without rocking, his arms crossed over his chest, as Mem scolded him. I waited, thinking they would start arguing at any time. But Datt just sat there, without rocking or saying anything. I played with blocks on the floor, one eye on Datt, as Mem's angry and impatient voice continued.

Suddenly, Datt jumped up from the rocking chair. His feet hit the floor in a shuffle. With wild and clumsy footsteps, he ran over to the hand sink. He bent over and pounded his head hard into the porcelain sink. To my horror, the top of his head broke off and lay there in the white sink. There was no blood, just the pale color of Datt's bald head, as it rocked back and forth like a bowl with a round bottom, its edges jagged, like a broken eggshell. Datt stood there with no top on his head and said angrily to Mem, "Now do you feel better?"

When I screamed myself awake, the horror and fear became a palpable thing in the room—something I could have reached out and touched, though I didn't dare. I couldn't hide or shrink from it, I couldn't beat it back, and I couldn't run from it. I was hot under the covers of the bed I shared with my sisters, Lizzie and Sarah. Mem came and stood over our bed and asked what the matter was. Between sobs, I stammered out what had happened in the dream. Mem said, "It was only a dream; now go back to sleep. I'll leave my door open so you can see the light." She tucked the covers around me and went back to bed. I couldn't say to Mem, "But it was just like real; maybe it could really happen." I looked at the dim light coming through the open door, and slowly the sobs turned into the hiccups that Mem called "sniffling." I couldn't push the horrible images out of my head. I wanted to go to sleep to escape it, and yet I was afraid of dreaming again. I tried thinking about something good, but everything inside me felt black. When I finally did fall asleep, it was mercifully a dreamless sleep.

I awoke in the early morning light as Mem was waking my older brother and sister, Joey and Lizzie, for school. The memory of the dream was more bearable than the dream had been.

There were other nights in my childhood that were frightening. The night "the Yankee" came into our house and disturbed the whole family, I wished I could awake and find it was all a dream—but it was all too real.

Datt was working up at the Hale Farm doing chores that summer. He carried milk from the barn to the milkhouse. During evening chores, Datt had a run-in with a man living in the area who was considered crazy. People shied away from him whenever possible. The Amish all called him "the Yankee" (Yankee was a term for someone who wasn't Amish). At dinner, Datt related the story of how when he was carrying milk, the Yankee had parked his car in the path between the barn and the milkhouse, so Datt asked (or most likely demanded) that the Yankee move his car. The Yankee refused, and an argument ensued in which Datt told him he had no right to make his job harder than it already was. I knew the Yankee because he came to buy eggs from Mem every week. He often smelled bad, and he had a demanding and demeaning way of treating Mem. Once he had the audacity to ask her to cook some eggs for him, and she would not say no. While she was getting out her cast iron skillet, he asked if she had ever cooked anything with lard in the pan, and she retorted, "Not since I washed it!" The Yankee reluctantly agreed to eat the eggs Mem fried for him.

The night Datt had the run-in with the Yankee, the air was hot and heavy in our bedroom. My nightdress stuck to me whenever I turned. I rolled back and forth, trying to find a comfortable position. Not only was I hot, but I had an uneasy feeling in the pit of my stomach.

Something rumbled in the distance, and then the walls of our room lit up. It was a car coming into our lane—in the middle of the night. I sat up in bed. The car stopped, the engine shut off, and the door banged.

"Simon!" a man's voice shouted. The fear I felt from that raspy voice calling Datt in the middle of the night made me lie back down very quickly—I wanted to disappear into the bed. It felt like my heart had stopped beating, yet I could hear it thundering in my ears. The voice called out again, this time louder—"Siiii-monn!" Then someone banged on the door.

"Everyone stay really quiet," I heard Mem whisper from their bedroom next door to ours.

I scooted closer to Lizzie. In the light from the car's headlights, I could see that her eyes were wide open and staring.

"Who is it?" I whispered to Mem through the open doorway between us.

"It's the Yankee. Shhhh!" she whispered back.

"Si-monn!" the man shouted at our dark house. The outside door creaked open and footsteps came up the stairs into the kitchen. Lizzie grabbed my hand under the covers, and Sarah made a little squeaking noise. I hoped Baby Susie, in Mem and Datt's room, would not wake up and cry. No sound came from Joey's room.

"Datt," Mem said in a low hiss, "go down and see what he wants!"

Datt said, "I'm not going down there. Just be quiet, and maybe he'll go away."

The Yankee didn't go away. First he rattled the handle on the water pail on the water stand and shouted Datt's name again. Then he walked over to the bottom of the stairway and opened the door. He yelled up, "Siii-monn!" Mem and Datt whispered some more, angrily.

Then I heard one of them get out of bed. I held my breath as I listened to Mem's footsteps going to the top of the stairs. She called down into the darkness: "What do you want?"

"Eggs!" the Yankee said.

Mem spoke again, and I could tell she was trying to sound calm, though I heard the trembling in her voice. "What did she say?" I whispered to Lizzie.

"You woke up the children," Lizzie whispered. "Come back tomorrow and I will give you the eggs."

The Yankee shouted something else. Lizzie translated: "I'm hungry and I can't sleep!"

Mem stepped down into the darkness of the stairway.

All I could think of was that this man could hurt Mem.

After what felt like a long time, I heard Mem say something out loud. She came up the stairs quickly and said to Datt, "I gave him two dozen eggs. Now if he doesn't go, you will have to deal with him!" She wasn't pretending to be calm any more, and her voice sounded scared. "He smells terrible. I think he's been drinking!"

The Yankee muttered something, and then we heard the door open and close. The car started, and its lights moved across the walls as he drove away. All became quiet again.

Mem came into our room.

"Why did he want eggs in the middle of the night?" I asked, sitting up and looking through the darkness at Mem.

"I don't know. Lie down, Lomie," she said, and pulled the sheet over me. I noticed her hands were shaking.

I lay down, but like the rest of the family, I could not sleep. I wondered if someone could die from being scared. It seemed as if the darkness that lived inside me could take over and erase me altogether.

First thing the next day, Datt went to the hardware store and bought two big aluminum brackets and nailed them on the inside frame of the outside door, and got a sturdy two-by-four to drop between them at night, barring the door. Lizzie gave a sigh of relief when she came home from school and saw it. At first I felt safer looking at it, too, knowing the Yankee couldn't come into our house in the middle of the night again. This was Datt's way of trying to protect us, but I also knew it was too late. What I discovered that night—that Datt could not be counted on to protect his family—was a reality that instilled fear in me long after I knew that the Yankee had moved out of town and would not disturb us again.

I kept thinking about that bar across the door, knowing it was too high up for me to reach. Instead of making me feel secure, the barred door made me feel trapped. Danger didn't just come from outside our house—it lurked in every corner.

The most disturbing aspect of the Yankee's intrusion into our home that night, though I did not know it at the time, was that my mother was very pregnant with my younger brother, Simon.

THE SOUND OF THE DOOR closing down the hall brought me back to the present. Other "Adas" were arriving at the Victorian house on Green Street for another week of studies at Smith College. I went down to the kitchen to make myself dinner. I warmed up leftovers from the dinner I had cooked with David the night before—steak, green beans with almonds, and rice pilaf. I was getting into the rhythm of a typical week at Smith—classes and homework during the week, and then returning home to Vermont to be with David for the weekend. I loved my world at Smith as much as I loved being with David, but my transition back to Smith was a bit harder because I missed David. We talked on the phone every day, but it wasn't the same as being with him.

I sat down at the end of the table in the common dining room to eat my dinner. I could see down into the kitchen of the Green Street Café next door. As I watched the movements of the people in the kitchen, my thoughts drifted back to Datt. I tried to remember how long he had remained in his depressed state of rocking and not working—as a child it had seemed like several years, but it might have been only one winter. There were certain times of the year when he would work, such as in the spring when he and Mem made maple syrup, and when he did chores on the Hale farm up the road from us.

I knew that Datt's mother had helped shape him into who he was. Both Grandmother's and Datt's medieval religious beliefs lived in a little black German book. Datt would take the book from the desk and settle into his rocking chair after supper. He would hold one of us on his lap and show us the pictures in the little black book, *Die Herzen der Menschen* (The Hearts of People). The book had pictures of men and hearts—with good and bad things representing what was in their hearts. As Datt showed us the pictures, he would say, "See—there is no room for both good and bad in our hearts. When the bad things come into our hearts, the good things have to leave." He pointed to the pictures to demonstrate. I once asked Datt, "How do we keep good things in our hearts?"

"We have to do the things God expects us to. Children need to obey their parents. Parents need to do what the church expects. If we do these things, God will reward us when we die," he said. Then he told me a story . . .

"Once our family made a big fire to burn *hecka* (brush) after my datt died. The fire burned hot, with flames reaching into the air far above our heads." Datt's voice became louder and his words came fast when he said, "Mem gathered all us children around her by the fire and said to us, 'This is a small fire compared to hell. Even if you were to burn in this fire, it would be nothing compared to the pain of the hell fire. Satan is ready to throw children into the fire with his pitchfork if they don't obey their parents.'

"My mem told us that for our own good," Datt said, finishing the story.

I slid off Datt's lap and realized I was more afraid of his mother than ever before. I asked Lizzie if she wanted to stack blocks with me.

The beliefs that Datt derived from the little black book influenced his way of thinking. If he truly believed that there was no room for both good and bad in his heart, he would have thought he had to be perfect to be good. Of course he was not perfect—in fact, on some level he probably knew he was less perfect than most—and so he worried that he was bad through and through, and most likely damned.

Grandmother used Datt's fears to control him. She wielded an unusual amount of influence on our family. It never made sense to me why Mem allowed Grandmother so much say in our family matters. I know that Mem felt sorry for Grandmother, but that still doesn't explain why she allowed Grandmother to make key decisions for our family. Once Grandmother arrived at our house as Mem had gotten back from grocery shopping. Grandmother went through all the groceries, telling Mem what she could have done without. When Mem told this story, she told it in a neutral voice. I asked her why she allowed Grandmother to do that, and she launched into stories about the hardships Grandmother had endured in her life.

When Grandmother was six years old, her mother died. Grandmother was the oldest child in her family. Her father remarried fairly quickly. Grandmother's stepmother sounded like she had walked out of the story of Hansel and Gretel—she was very cruel to Grandmother.

Whenever the stories of Grandmother as a child didn't get the desired effect, Mem would tell us about the hardships Grandmother endured as an adult—how she lost her husband during the Great Depression, with five children and another one on the way. Even though the family could grow most of its own food, they still needed some money for buying other things. Grandmother had the back-breaking job of digging potatoes for a dollar per day.

It didn't matter how many times Mem told us these stories, I was too scared of Grandmother to feel sorry for her. She was so stern, she didn't even like it when we laughed or giggled, and she didn't like it when we saw our reflections in the mirror. She believed that as soon as a child knew what a comb was for, then the child was old enough to be spanked. And she firmly believed that Amish girls should play with homemade faceless cloth dolls, and not the plastic ones with faces. Other Amish girls could play with real plastic dolls, but Grandmother and her sidekick, Aunt Katie, who only reinforced Grandmother, were stricter than any other Amish people I knew. It seemed to me that Aunt Katie was training to be just like Grandmother when she grew old. Both were tall and thin and had long hawk noses. Age was the biggest difference between them—Grandmother was the kind of person who I imagined had always been old, and Aunt Katie only needed some more years to get there.

Grandmother and Aunt Katie brought their very own darkness with them when they visited us as a pair. Everything around them was black—the buggy, the horse, and their clothing—giving their already severe demeanor and outlook more emphasis. They had appeared on the morning after one of my most frightening childhood memories.

My sisters and I had been sitting at the table, eating bread and milk before going to bed. The oil lamp cast a faint yellow light around the kitchen, and rain drummed on the windowsill outside. The pungent, smoky smell of the oil lamp lingered throughout the house. Mem was preparing us for bed. Datt was sleeping in the rocking chair in the living room. We could hear Datt snoring as the floorboards above us creaked with the weight of Mem carrying Baby Simon to bed. She came down the stairs, through the dark living room, and then she stepped into the kitchen doorway. She nearly filled the doorway with her wide hips. She had our sleeping caps in her hand, and suddenly she squeezed them very hard as she gasped and cried out. My sisters and I gaped with open mouths, our spoons halfway to our mouths. We watched help-lessly as Mem reached up with both arms, as if she was grasping at air, and then she dropped face down onto the floor in the kitchen doorway—Thud! Everything became still—there was only the sound of the rain dripping onto the windowsill outside. We were all too shocked to move. Then Joey, who was upstairs, suddenly came running down the stairs, and Datt awoke and scrambled towards Mem and kneeled next to her. He looked up and said, "Joey, go to the Sykoras and tell them to call the ambulance!" He called my mother's name, "Kettie!" and tried to rouse her. She did not wake up. He half-carried and half-dragged her onto the couch in the living room. He looked around and said, "Girls, go to bed!" We fled up the stairs to our beds. I lay on my back, breathing hard, too scared to move or talk.

When Joey came back from the Sykoras, he came upstairs and stood at his window and stared outside. Downstairs there were strange voices and banging noises. I wondered what was happening. All at once Joey cried out, "I think Mem is dying! They are taking her in a stretcher to the ambulance!" He ran through our room, then Mem and Datt's bedroom, and down the stairs. I wanted to cry, but I was too scared to. I had only a vague notion of what dying was, but the panic in Joey's voice conveyed the seriousness of the situation. My sisters and I got up and looked out our window as the ambulance drove slowly down our lane, carrying our mother away. I listened to the sound of the gravel crunching under the tires of the white station wagon, and I wondered whether Mem would ever come back.

The next morning, Lizzie and I figured out by the sounds coming from the kitchen that Aunt Katie was making breakfast instead of Mem. We dreaded going downstairs, but we also knew that if we got up too late, Grandmother and Aunt Katie would shame us for it. So, we tiptoed down the stairs and stood in the kitchen doorway. Grandmother sat at the table, spooning oatmeal into Baby Simon's mouth. Aunt Katie was making pancakes and eggs over the cookstove in her usual *shusslich* (clumsy) manner. When she saw us in the doorway, she said, "Lizzie, come set the table! Lomie, take your thumb out of your mouth!" She turned and stomped towards the table with a stack of pancakes. I went and picked up my doll from the toy box for comfort in place of sucking my thumb, but before breakfast was over, Aunt Katie took my doll away from me and I never saw her again.

It was Grandmother who told Mem and Datt not to tell us children why Mem had been taken to the hospital. When Datt came home the next morning, looking more tired than I'd ever seen him, he hung his hat on the peg on the wall next to the stairway. I came up behind him and asked, "When is Mem coming home with the baby?" I was going by what Joey said—that the reason mothers go to the hospital is to buy a baby. Datt walked by me and didn't answer. The dejected look on his face silenced me. I wondered if Mem was going to come home at all.

She did come home several days later, but she didn't bring a baby with her. I thought maybe Mem had really been sick instead of going to the hospital to "buy" a baby. A few days after she came home, Mem stood in the living room, holding a clear pump with a red ball over her breast. She squeezed the ball, and milk flowed into the pump as tears fell quietly down her cheeks. I touched her arm and asked her what was wrong. She only looked out the window towards the far end of the field on the other side of the road and shook her head. I wanted so much to make her feel better, but all I could do was watch her cry.

I had completely forgotten these events until I was in my early teens and we were visiting my cousin's gravesite. We were with Aunt Lizzie and my cousins Marie and Maudie. Aunt Lizzie had had four stillborn children, and she was standing by their graves. They were all lined up in a row, the little gravestones simply saying, "Stillborn Daughter [or Son] of Albert and Lizzie Kuntz," along with the dates.

Mem walked over to the row of pine trees that was the border between the graveyard and Uncle Ervin's farm. There she knelt by a little gravestone. I walked over and looked at it: "Stillborn Son of Simon S. Miller."

"Mem," I said, "I didn't know you had lost a child."

"Sure you did," she said and stood up briskly. "You remember when we had a baby that died, don't you? It was after Simon was born and before Katherine."

"Why didn't you tell us?"

"Grandmother told Datt and me it would be better not to tell you children."

I asked, "But why does this gravestone only have Datt's name and not yours?"

"Datt made a mistake. But don't say anything about it."

Aunt Lizzie called to Mem, and she walked away. I stood still, staring down at the little gravestone I had never even known was there before, feeling hollow and sad. If I had only known what had happened when I was a child, it could have been so much less confusing and frightening. Grandmother's stern dominance of Mem and Datt had not allowed us to know the simple truth—that the baby we expected she would bring home from the hospital had died.

I HEARD FOOTSTEPS coming up the stairs and realized I'd been sitting at the kitchen table, staring out the window for a long time. It was time to go and collect my mail from the Campus Center. I headed up to my room for my keys, and then down two flights of stairs to the street level. The fresh autumn air smelled good as I headed across campus. I kept thinking about Grandmother and wondering what my father would have been like if he had grown up with a different mother. Brother Joe once said that he would much rather have had Datt for a father than Grandmother for a mother. I was in my early teens at the time, and I couldn't have imagined a parent worse than my father. But Joe had a point—just having her for a grandmother was quite bad enough.

I remembered the day my fear of her had turned into hate.

I HAD BEEN GIVEN a doll as a gift from someone who noticed that I took good care of Sister Katherine when she was a baby. She was my favorite doll—she had a knob on her back that made her arms and legs move, and she had blue eyes that closed when I laid her down. She had a soft cloth body that made her feel more like a real baby than regular plastic dolls.

One day, when I was about eight years old, Grandmother and Aunt Katie drove into the lane. Mem said quietly, "Girls, go hide your dolls!" I stuck Heidi behind the couch. As it turned out, the hiding place was not good enough. When they left at the end of the day, my doll was nowhere to be found. A few days later, I found the top of her burned head in the pile of leaves in the woods. I felt the part of my heart that I thought should have loved my aunt and my grandmother turn to stone. I imagined my grandmother's body, tall and thin, clothed in a black dress, lying in a coffin. My mother thought it was a sin to wish someone dead, but I could not help it. I had never known such a feeling as what burned in my chest that day as I ran deep into the woods and screamed and sobbed out my fear and hatred of black-widow Grandmother.

Several years later, Grandmother and Aunt Katie moved to Wisconsin, and they only visited us once in a while after that. Uncle Sam's and Uncle Gid's families had already moved to Cashton, Wisconsin, where a new Amish settlement had been started with people moving from our community and from Iowa. The Cashton community was stricter than our own. After the uncles and their families and Grandmother and Aunt Katie had all moved out, they put a great deal of pressure on Mem and Datt to move their family to Cashton, too. It was one of the only times I was glad that Datt was so attached to his land. Even though I always had a fantasy about moving, I knew I didn't want to move to a stricter community, and I sure didn't want to be near Grandmother and Aunt Katie.

Grandmother was in her seventies the last time she traveled to Ohio. My uncles and aunts had also traveled from Wisconsin and New York State for a family reunion. She made a big point of telling all of us that this was to be her last trip, implying that she was then going back to Wisconsin to die soon thereafter.

The uncles got to joking the night everyone got together at our house. They all had a quick sense of humor, and they fed off one another. Some of us were crying from laughing so hard. Mem's bosom bounced as she laughed her quiet laugh that reddened her face. Even Datt, who was usually the last to laugh, was showing his toothless gums in exuberant laughter. I looked at Grandmother to see whether she was laughing. Sure enough, there was a smile playing at the corners of her mouth. Then she suddenly looked very serious and said, "You all are going to cry just as hard as you are laughing right now!" Uncle Gid said, "Well, I hope it will be as much fun!" The uncles bantered about a bit more, but the mood was lost. Grandmother had managed to smother the fun as effectively as if she had thrown a blanket over it.

Grandmother was right—this was her last trip to Ohio, but she didn't die for another twenty years.

Datt's obsession with death was something else Grandmother passed on to him. And they had a similar outlook on life in the sense that they seemed to have the fatalistic attitude that life happens to you, and there isn't anything you can do about it. They both expected the worst out of life, and they both got the worst out of life. Grandmother prolonged her death—we kept hearing she was on her way out for five years before she finally died, at ninety-four years old. Now, ten years later, Datt was finally reaching the end of his life, the moment he had been practicing for his whole life long.

WHEN I GOT BACK to my room, I thought about studying more for my German class the next day, but I was too distracted. I prepared for bed, sat down on my hickory rocker with a book, but I couldn't concentrate. I put it aside and snuggled into bed. I thought about how my fear of Datt had changed over the years. Part of the nature of my fear of him as a child was that I knew there was something wrong with Datt's mind, though I still didn't have words for "mental illness." And to this day I don't know what changed in Datt to make him go from being depressed to becoming intermittently depressed and violent. As each of us children became older and showed signs of developing our independence, he started to resort to violence, and my fears became reality.

Joe, being the oldest, was the first target of Datt's rage. I remember a beating Datt gave Joe when he was about fifteen years old. In the double doorway between the dining room and the living room, Datt whipped Joe with a belt, hard, so that Joe's heels came off the floor with each crack across his backside. Normally Datt whipped until we cried, and then he'd stop. We had learned to cry immediately. This time Joe stuck his hands in his pockets and refused to cry. I had been drying dishes at the counter. I wondered how he could stand it. When Joe didn't cry after several hits, Datt grabbed onto the belt with both hands and cracked it across Joe's back, nearly knocking him off his feet. Joe's white face was set in stone. Then all of a sudden his knees buckled and he fell to the floor.

Frozen with fear, I couldn't utter a sound. My memory of what happened next has completely vanished. It is as if I saw only part of a film. Perhaps my mind was protecting itself in not recording the level of fear I felt.

It was the last time Joe took a beating from Datt without fighting back. From the time he was sixteen to the time he left home, Joe and Datt had physical fights—once in a barn where a church service was being held, with other men around. The bishop's son was among those witnessing the fight. He looked at the other men and said, "Shouldn't we be doing something about this?"

When Joe left home to get married, we sighed in relief, thinking that would be the end of Datt's violence. But instead of ending, his violence was now turned on the girls as each of us reached the age of normal adolescent rebellion.

I find it surprising that Datt did not get into the habit of hitting Mem. I remember him hitting her only once. The two of them were arguing out in the yard when he turned and punched her in the chest, just once, and then drew his hand back, as if it had betrayed him. Most of the time, even in his rages he seemed to have the self-control not to hit her. Sister Susan remembers another time, when we were sitting at the supper table, when Datt hit Mem. Joe, who was in his late teens at the time, stood up and told Datt that he would never hit Mem again—or else he, Joe, would hit Datt back. Susan attributes the fact that Datt didn't habitually hit Mem to Joe's standing up to Datt. I am not so sure. I think that on some level, Datt knew the difference between hitting his daughters, who in his mind he was "disciplining"—and hitting Mem. He knew he could not survive without her.

I AWOKE TO A SERIES of loud bangs right outside my window. It was the garbage truck emptying the dumpster. I looked at my clock and wondered why they had to do it so early in the morning—it was just after 6:00 A.M. I tried to go back to sleep, but I suddenly remembered Datt, and how I still had to decide whether to stay at Smith or travel to Ohio. I asked myself what I would regret if I did not go visit him. Then I realized that I might not have any regrets, because in the past fifteen years, I had established a relationship with Datt that I knew was as good as it was going to get. It was difficult to achieve this, because the rest of the family did not see Datt as a person—whenever they visited, they talked with Mem, and everyone ignored Datt altogether. Over the years, my siblings had, in different degrees, bought into the myth that Mem had created, that Datt was a complete failure as our parent and as a person, while Mem could do no wrong. I found it was not so clear-cut: Datt's good attributes were ignored in the same way that Mem's faults were unrecognized. In my view, one of her faults was to ignore Datt when we visited—she actually treated him as if he were a piece of furniture. Sometimes she went as far as talking about Datt in front of him, as if he were not there.

I wanted to change this pattern of treating Datt like a nonperson. During one of my visits home, I asked Datt about his railroad days, and he became all animated, and motioned as he spoke, telling me how his head had gotten caught between two train cars. One of the people he worked with saw what had happened and alerted the engineer, who pulled the cars forward, freeing Datt's head.

Mem's reaction to my new behavior was interesting. She interrupted and said, "Datt, that's not how it happened . . . !"

I asked Mem, "Were you there?"

"No, but that's not how he told me the story . . ."

As soon as Mem interrupted, Datt stopped rocking in his bent hickory rocker, with his feet crossed, and listened meekly.

I knew Mem wanted me to ask her how he had told the story before, which would have brought the conversation back to the way she was used to—with her doing the talking, and he being the nonperson. I didn't ask her. Instead I said, "Mem, let him talk."

Datt took up his story where he had left off.

I wasn't that surprised when Mem burst into tears, for I had always known that Mem used her tears to manipulate people's sympathies. I ignored her and kept my focus on what Datt was saying.

When Mem saw I wasn't responding, she dried her crocodile tears and sat on her hands and pouted.

David and I engaged Datt in conversations after that, and we brought him maple popcorn from the Log Cabin in Burton, where he used to sell his maple syrup. Whenever I wrote Mem a letter, I also wrote to Datt. He wrote back, even though his handwriting looked like he was still in the fifth grade, which was the last year of school he had completed, and some of the letters were not that coherent—but I felt honored that he wrote them, all the same. Then in one letter, he had clearly stopped writing in mid-sentence. The letter made no sense, and I knew his letter-writing days were probably over.

In this process of seeing Datt for who he was, I found I had forgiven him. To fully forgive him, I needed to understand how he could have committed the wrongs he did. With his mental illness and with his level of intelligence, perhaps he could not have made different choices than the ones he made. This was borne out when his violence ceased after he began to take medication for his illness twenty-five years ago. I could not hold him as responsible as someone who was intelligent and deliberately set out to hurt others.

I STRETCHED AND LOOKED out over the roof of the science building. I felt like I needed to pinch myself to make sure I was awake, because sometimes it was almost too much to grasp that I was realizing my lifelong dream of attending college.

It was soon time for my ethics class, in which we were discussing Plato, one of my favorite philosophers. The professor had an unassuming style, outfitted in his Birkenstocks and flannel shirts. He had a way of examining issues that invited us to turn them around and look at them from all sides. I found this approach liberating, and I looked forward to each one of his classes.

As I stood under the warm shower, I remembered the magic of my very first class at Smith. It was astronomy, and the professor, who is from Pakistan, had put up a slide on the overhead projector of a child sitting on a sandy beach. He started out the class by saying, in his lilting accent, that there are more galaxies in the universe than there are grains of sand on earth. He also said that scientists today do not know whether the universe is finite or infinite. "But," he said, "we do know that there are an infinite number of mysteries in the universe." I had the feeling as I sat in this class that my mind was expanding, so that it could absorb all these incredible ideas I was being exposed to. This was the world in which I belonged, the same way Datt was in the world in which he belonged, surrounded by family members and people from his Amish community. I decided that I would stay at Smith for now and travel back for his funeral. I knew that the reason I could make this decision with a clear conscience is because I had made peace with him. I breathed a prayer of gratitude for this blessing.

Good works are links that form a chain of love.
MOTHER TERESA

A Frolic

ater that same day as I walked across campus, I called Sister Susan. We had been emailing back and forth constantly since Datt had gone into the hospital and subsequently gone back home. Susan said Datt was doing about the same as he had been, although they were now giving him morphine every four hours to relieve his coughing. She said that he was sometimes aware, and other times he wasn't.

"Speaking of being aware, I was thinking again of what Datt said to you and Sarah when you two visited him in the hospital."

"You mean when he said he felt bad that 'you girls are not going to get an inheritance'?"

"Yes. That took a tremendous amount of awareness, which I didn't think he was capable of. First of all, even if he was aware of what that meant to us, I would have thought he wouldn't care that we aren't going to end up with much of an inheritance because we left the Amish. But the most amazing thing to me is that it's the kind of thing that fathers think about when they're dying. I didn't think Datt had any paternal feelings for his children. It seems like he does in this case. And not only that, but I would have thought because all of us girls have left the Amish, he wouldn't want us to have any inheritance, even if he had paternal feelings for us."

"I know! I cannot tell you how surprised Sarah and I were by that. Did I tell you what Mem's reaction was when we mentioned that?"

"I don't think you did."

"She got really defensive. She said, 'But you *are* getting an inheritance. Joe and Emma have been paying into an account for that all along!'"

"Interesting. Why do you think she was so defensive?"

"I don't know. I wondered the same thing."

"Do you know if there will be any inheritance at all, or what the plan is for that?"

"You once told me that Joe and Emma are paying into an account to pay for the farm, but I don't know much more than that."

"Yes, Mem told me that Joe and Emma were buying the property from them for thirty thousand dollars, and that they are paying that into an account that will be disbursed to the rest of us for inheritance. But I have no idea whether Joe and Emma are keeping up with that, and also I think they have to take from this fund for expenses for Mem and Datt."

"I suppose time will tell. Oh, by the way, did I tell you that one of the nurses asked Datt who his favorite child was?"

"No, you didn't. Why would someone ask such a question?"

"Maybe she figured if you can't ask that question now, you never can. We all do have our favorites, I suppose."

"I don't think so. I could never choose which of my sons is my favorite."

"Anyway, can you guess who he said was his favorite?"

I thought for a moment. "Most likely Sarah."

"Yup. That was predictable, wasn't it?"

"It sure was. It confirms what we already knew, though."

"Yes, it does. And I don't think it would have made any difference to him to know that Sarah often did things against his will as much as you and I did, but she was just much sneakier about it. Do you remember the time she climbed out the window?"

"What window?"

"The upstairs window. Do you remember how Datt would just decide we couldn't go out some nights? On this particular Saturday night, Sarah was all dressed up, ready to go out. She came downstairs, and Datt said to her, 'Sarah, I don't want you going out tonight.' So she said, 'Okay' and went back upstairs, where she opened up the window and climbed down the ladder she had put there for that purpose. The next morning when Datt said to Sarah, 'Thank you for obeying last night,' she casually said, 'You're welcome.'"

"How sneaky!"

"I know. And do you know that when she and I recently talked about that, she actually defended her approach, and said we should have learned the same tactics to keep ourselves out of trouble?"

"She did? But where is the honesty in that? I guess she and I have a different idea of what's ethical. In Datt's eyes, Sarah could do no wrong, and the rest of us could do no right. I realize now that the reason you and I played such a tug-of-war with Sarah is that the only way we could get approval from Mem or Datt was through her. So that awful triangle we had going was our roundabout route to parental approval. I wish we could get to the point in our adult lives where we are all close. I think part of the present situation of you and me being closer, while we feel distant from Sarah, is that we've taken a different path from the one Sarah has chosen. We are both pursuing our education, and she is surrounding herself with young children, which doesn't lend itself to getting a formal education."

"She claims she is happy, so I wish her the best," Susan said.

"I do too. I just keep asking her when she is going to stop taking in foster children if she ends up adopting the children she takes in."

"She is very sensitive about that."

"I know. It certainly is her decision. I suppose she might say she doesn't see how our pursuits of education are meaningful. But it sure is meaningful to me. I worked long and hard to get to college, and Susan, this is better than I ever imagined. Every one of my classes is so wonderful, I cannot imagine this being better than it is!"

"I am so glad. And here I am at a rinky-dink community college–type place. I wish I could do what you're doing. If only my children were older . . ."

"Hey, at least you are going to school. When you become a lawyer and you find your dream job, the school you went to won't matter."

"I do like my classes, even if this isn't a high-caliber school. But listen, I have to go. I need to get Grace to bed, and get off to bed myself. I have to clean two houses tomorrow."

"Okay, I'll talk with you later. Let's stay in touch via email."

"Good idea."

I TALKED WITH DAVID every day. On this night, I called and he had just finished eating dinner. I asked him if it was strange living by himself.

"I'm getting used to it," David said.

"I keep thinking how weird it is that in July, Paul, Tim, and I were all living there, and now you're all by yourself, slaving away to keep us all in school. Have you heard how Tim is doing at Johnson State College, by the way?"

"Yeah, he seems to be doing all right. He wants his mattress from his bed, because he says his is really uncomfortable."

"You're not going to take it to him, are you?"

"Why not?"

"First of all, I don't want it ruined, and second of all, if the mattress is that bad, he should ask the school to provide him with a different one. But you are the sole parent in charge now that I'm away, and there is nothing I can do about it if you decide to bring his up there."

David asked, "So, how are your classes going?" I hesitated. I recognized David's tendency to change the subject to distract me from disagreeing with him. But I'd also learned that trying to stick to a subject he didn't want to talk about was futile, so I answered his question.

"They're going well. I had my triple E class this morning."

"What's your triple E class?"

"Ethics with Ernie at Eight."

"Oh, you told me about that class. You're discussing Plato's Forms."

"Yes. My classes are going well, but I seem to have a hard time concentrating on my homework, knowing what is going on with Datt. People keep asking me if I'm going to go see him before he dies," I said.

"You have decided not to, right?"

"Yes. If I hadn't come to an understanding with him back when the boys were young, I might feel the need to, but I honestly feel I have accepted him for exactly who he is."

"I agree. I don't think the rest of your siblings have this understanding. I think things are as they should be—the people who need to be there for your father are already there."

"And I am where I need to be."

"That's what I think. But I'm going to go watch a movie, and I bet you have studying to do."

"Yes, I do. I miss you."

"Already? You were just here yesterday."

"Yes, already. The only thing wrong with this Smith education is that you and I can't live together."

"That doesn't stop us from having fun on weekends, does it?"

"So far, no. Having our sex limited to the weekends doesn't make it any less intense," I whispered.

"Can your roommates hear you say that?" David laughed.

"Maybe. Does that embarrass you somehow?"

"You're the one who should be embarrassed."

"You think I should be? I'm not."

"Okay, I better go. Otherwise you really are going to embarrass me."

"I'm going to embarrass you even though you're all by yourself?"

"No, but I bet I will meet your housemates someday soon. Then I will be embarrassed."

"Okay, good night. I love you."

"Love you too."

IN A PHONE CONVERSATION with Susan one night, she and I fantasized about taking a German class together, and then she broke into the language of our childhood. Susan could still converse and understand everything said in the Amish language, which is a dialect of German often known as Pennsylvania Dutch. This dialect originated in Europe, but as each new generation incorporated more English words in the United States, the dialect has become increasingly more of a mishmash of German and English. I understood what Susan was saying, but I could not answer her back, because I have lost much of my vocabulary over the years since I left. For many years, when I visited my home community, I could slip right back into the language. Then I didn't go back for nearly three years, so when I next visited Mem and Datt, I found it harder to converse in Amish. I have incrementally lost more of the dialect each year, to the point where I can understand most of it, but I cannot respond in kind. Susan noticed I was stumped and said, "So, maybe there is something I am better at than you."

"Of course, lots of things," I said.

Later I thought about what Susan had said, and decided to write her an email. I pointed out that she is good at many things, and I didn't think it was productive to compare. I wrote, "In short, I hope you don't feel inferior to me. I accept that I have talents, including the ability to reason, which is what God gave us that He didn't give to the other animals. Part of the reason I am coming into my own is because I have come to accept myself for who I am. I no longer try to be like others, or envy who they are, because I like my life and who I am. I hope that you can also come to that place. The difference between you and me is like comparing an apple with a peach. One is not better than the other, but rather they are good in their own right. I love you for who you are, and I love myself for who I am, the same way I love both peaches and apples."

That night I remembered how my relationship with Susan had been tumultuous all through our childhood and teenage years. Then, the competition was downright fierce between us because neither of us knew how to temper it—in fact, that ferocity often came out in physical fights. One of our fights happened on a Sunday morning, when we were both getting ready for church. I was combing my hair in front of the mirror in the bedroom we shared. There were three bedrooms and four sisters still living at home at the time. Lizzie had moved in with her friend Amanda when she turned twenty-one. I had a room by myself for a time at the far north end of the house, with a window facing the sugarhouse. One Saturday, when I came home from cleaning house for one of the "English" families I worked for, I found Susan had moved into my room. There had been no discussion, and she refused to discuss it now that she was already moved in. I wondered why, if she really hated me as much as she let on, she would even consider moving into my room.

On this Sunday morning, as I stood by the mirror, combing my hair, Susan came up and also stood in front of the mirror to comb her hair. I moved to the side, giving her half the space in front of the mirror and not an inch more. Our elbows kept clashing, but I stood my ground and ignored her. I thought I would be safe—Susan's style was to hold her own when a fight was about to start, and make the other person hit first. I was determined not to this time.

Suddenly, Susan shoved me hard and said, "Move over!" I was not ready for her shove, so it threw me off base and I landed on the floor, up against the bed. I stood up and shoved her back, hard. She landed on the floor behind the door. I saw the anger sparking in her eyes as she got up. She grabbed onto my hair and pulled as hard as she could. I pulled at her hair, I hit, and I scratched. In the end, when Mem came up to stop the fight, Susan had a whole handful of hair wound around her hand, and I had a round, bare spot on the top of my head. I had skin under my fingernails from her arm.

I thought I could use my bald spot as a reason for not going to church—at the time we looked for any excuses we could find to skip church—but Mem and Datt insisted I had to go. The burning and stinging from the spot where the hair had been pulled out by its roots lasted all day.

How appropriate that Susan and I had fought over space in front of the mirror, each claiming space for the kind of self-reflection denied to us by our family and community. Now I was grateful that she and I were coming to terms with who and what we were, leaving behind those nasty disputes of our childhood.

My DAILY PATTERN of studying, having meals with the women in the house, and staying in touch with David and Susan became routine. So did the childhood memories as I lay down to sleep at night.

There was a time when the poverty was the keenest in my childhood, when Datt was in his worst depression and we still lived in the little tiny house that was bursting with eight people. This was before Katherine was born. I still don't know how Mem was able to feed and clothe a family of six children while also earning most of the money. She sewed suits for the Amish men in the community. With this money and the earnings from maple syrup in the spring and selling eggs from the farm, Mem somehow fed and clothed us.

Our chicken feed came in 100-pound cotton feedbags. Many people washed these and made kitchen towels out of them. The cotton was soft, and the towels were absorbent. When money was scarcest in the family, Mem sewed underwear for us from these cotton feedbags, and also dyed the cotton and made dresses.

As I became old enough to notice, I felt as though the dysfunction in our family was a public affair—everyone in the community knew about it, but they did little to help in any ongoing way. Perhaps they didn't know how, or perhaps they felt that because Mem was a responsible parent, the children wouldn't suffer. But most likely, our family didn't get the help it needed because the Amish aid system often does not apply to people who don't work hard to help themselves. At some point, I realized our family was serving a purpose within the community—we were used as an example of what could go wrong if one was lazy, didn't help oneself, or didn't properly adhere to the Amish ways. This allowed other families to be *gut oh tzene* (well regarded), while we provided the contrasting bad example. Any problems within these righteous families remained private because the focus stayed on what was going wrong within families such as our own.

I was never able to figure out precisely how each person's or family's standing in the community was determined, because it seemed so arbitrary—it had more to do with who a person was, rather than how that person behaved. Once a family has a bad reputation, it is extremely hard to improve it. And the reverse is also true—good reputations die hard.

I believe that Datt's standing would have been somewhat improved had the tragedy of his father's death not occurred when Datt was thirteen years old. Datt's father was *gut oh tzene*—a successful farmer with a beautiful matched team of horses, a kind man, and a responsible father. When he became ill with appendicitis, they called the local doctor to come to the house. This doctor had a reputation for being rough, and in this case, he lived up to his reputation. When he pushed on my grandfather's abdomen, my grandfather felt the appendix rupture. He was in excruciating pain for two days and then he died, leaving five children behind with another one on the way in the middle of the Depression. Datt was the oldest. He never accepted his father's death, most likely because he suffered so greatly from the consequences of it. He had to go live on a farm for his room and board when he was a mere thirteen years old. So not only was Datt considered simple, but he also missed out on any self-confidence and skills he might have gained from his father's continued guidance at an important stage in his development. In a closed community, this lack of self-confidence is seized upon—the people at the top stay there by putting others down. And the ones near the bottom see this and join in on the belittling, hoping they might improve their own standing.

When Datt was in his late teens, he worked on a potato farm. There was an Amish woman working there who, like Datt, was physically strong and more stubborn than intelligent. Her nickname was Queen. She and Datt disagreed one day in the potato house, where they were both supposed to be sorting potatoes, and she promptly hit him and knocked him out. The other Amish who worked on the farm teased him constantly, and this incident gave them fodder. Years later, Datt was unhappy with who Sister Sarah married, because he was the grandson of one of Datt's worst tormentors from that era. Datt had a long memory for the people who had wronged him.

There is another factor that determined one's place within the community, and that had to do with performance: ambitious people and hard workers gained respect, but anyone who was considered simple, lazy, or shifty didn't—regardless of mitigating factors such as depression or any other mental illness. The Amish way was to "shame" the person into working harder and helping himself—and likewise, if someone was simple, he should just "smarten up." So instead of trying to help Datt improve his situation, the people in the community shamed him. He was still included in all the community events, but the Amish have a way of both including and isolating someone at the same time. This system of approval and disapproval often works, forcing people to step into the prescribed and "normal" behavior expected within the community. Once in a while, a person cannot change in the ways the community requires. However, the pressure to conform never ceases, and so in this way, the person—a person like Datt—feels like an outsider within the community all his life.

As far as Mem's reputation was concerned, she made her mistake when she married Datt. It is still a mystery as to why she did marry him. The story goes that she was an "old maid" when Datt came to her to have his suit made. From putting the pieces together, I realize this took place when he was making his return to the community. Even after the suit was finished, he continued to visit her. They began dating, and eventually they set plans to get married. At some point in this relationship, Mem's father had a talk with her and warned her not to marry Datt. I often wonder if he was concerned about her standing and reputation in the community, for he and his family were *gut oh tzene*.

For whatever reason, Mem did end up marrying Datt. It seemed that our family's reputation was sealed before any of us children were even born. When we were growing up, the people in the community did not let us forget that we were just "Sim's children" (Datt's Amish name was Sim).

Even though the Amish people didn't help my family financially or in an ongoing way, they did help in customary ways, such as the "frolic" that helped lay the foundation for an addition to our house.

The house we lived in until I was five years old had four rooms in it—a kitchen and living room downstairs, and two bedrooms upstairs. Then when Joe was seven, my uncle came and put a partition wall in the second bedroom, creating a tiny room for Joe to sleep in, making it three bedrooms upstairs. There were six children and two adults living in this little house. On those occasions when Mem would ask Datt what we were going to do about our tiny house, he would answer with *"Ach, ich wess net"* (Oh, I don't know).

Then one night at the supper table, the conversation turned from the abstract to the specific. While we were eating corn on the cob, and Mem was cutting Datt's corn off the cob, she said that Dodde (Grandfather) had stopped in at the Herrings and asked them about that old house on their property, and that they were willing to sell it for fifty dollars.

Datt didn't say much about the plan other than it would be cheaper than lumber. This must have been all Mem needed, because she and Dodde started to make plans. As it turned out, they paid the Herrings two hundred dollars instead of fifty dollars, but Mem said it was still a lot cheaper than putting up a new house.

Datt started digging the hole for the cellar with a shovel and wheelbarrow, under Dodde's direction. Each evening, Datt would eat supper, then dig a few more wheelbarrows full of dirt out of the cellar hole before going to bed early. Each day when I came home from school, the hole would be bigger than the day before. I wondered how it was that Datt could work so hard, when he had been sitting on his rocking chair for so long. Maybe he only worked hard when he thought there was a reason to. He did not want to spend the money on a backhoe to dig out the hole for the basement.

I was in kindergarten at the time. One afternoon, as the school bus came around the bend towards home, one of the children pointed and said, "Look, what is that?"

I looked out the front window of the bus and saw the old Herring house on top of a long truck, sitting in the Sykoras' lane. As we got closer, I saw what I thought was the chimney of the house suddenly wave. My mouth dropped open. It was Datt, sitting on top of the house, next to the chimney!

The children in the bus chattered excitedly. I realized that Mrs. Heitman, our driver, couldn't turn the bus around the same way she usually did, because the truck with the house on it was in the way. I got up out of my seat and said to her, "Oh, you can turn down this road and then back into our lane!"

Mrs. Heitman chuckled and said, "Yes, honey, I can do that."

I found Mem standing in the yard in front of the chicken coop, with Sarah, Susie, and Baby Simon. I went over and stood with them. We watched as Dodde and three other Amish men directed the driver of the truck to back the Herring house up to our house. I looked at Datt way up on top of the house and hoped he wouldn't fall down.

"Why is Datt up there?" I asked.

"Someone had to ride up there to hold up the electric lines when the house went under them," Mem said.

I gasped. "I thought nobody was supposed to touch them!"

Mem smiled and said, "Don't worry; they turned off the electricity."

I watched Dodde directing everyone with hand signals. When the old house was up against our house, the truck driver turned off the engine. In the sudden quiet, I heard Dodde call, "Well done!"

Then someone put a ladder up to the roof, and Datt climbed down from his perch with a big grin on his face.

The men built block towers under each corner of the house. Then they turned a big metal wheel, and slowly the house began rising up off the truck. When the house was no longer sitting on the truck, but on the block towers, the driver started up the truck and slowly drove it out from under the house. Mem explained that the house was going to stay on those blocks until the cellar walls were built, and then they would use the jack to let the house down onto the new foundation.

MEM WOKE US UP EARLY the next morning for the frolic, or work party. When we were finished eating, Mem said, "Lizzie and Lomie, do the dishes and sweep the floor. As soon as you've finished that, go and pick the corn and the tomatoes. Sarah, you play with Susie, and let's hope Baby Simon sleeps a while longer."

Mem and Datt had gotten up early to butcher chickens, and now Mem fried them on all four burners of the oil stove. The smell made my stomach growl, even though I'd just eaten a big bowl of oatmeal. We had set up the church benches the night before under the trees next to the woodshed, where it would be shady and away from the dirt.

"Joey," Mem said, "I need you to go and bury the chicken leavings back in the woods. Hurry up—people will be coming any minute."

Lizzie and I had just started picking corn when the first buggy drove up. "It's Momme and Dodde," Lizzie said. She was close to the edge of the cornfield, so I went and peeked out between the cornstalks with her. Dodde was short and stout, with a twinkle in his eye. He looked like Mem would look if she were older and a man instead of a woman. Momme was short and plump, but not as big as Mem or most of my aunts. She was as mild-mannered as my other grandmother was severe. She walked into the house carrying two big baskets covered with white towels. Datt helped Dodde unhitch the horse and water him at the trough by the pump, and then tied him to a tree by the woodshed. Dodde walked over to the cellar hole and stood looking down, hooking his thumbs into his suspenders and chewing slowly on his tobacco. After a moment, he spit a stream of brown juice onto the ground and then wiped his beard. Lizzie and I looked at each other and wrinkled our noses. But we liked Dodde. He would say funny things to make people laugh, and he liked to tease Momme. Even though she pretended to be angry, she would be laughing.

Next, a van drove into the yard, and several of Mem's sisters and their families got out. They had come all the way from Mesopotamia, eleven miles away, in a hired van. I recognized Aunt Lizzie and Uncle Bert, Aunt Sarah and Uncle Dan, and the aunt who shared a name with me, Saloma, and her husband, Ervin. They had brought some of the cousins, but they couldn't all fit in one van, so the older ones had to stay home. Marie and Maudie came, and they were almost the same age as Lizzie and me.

More people arrived, some by buggy and some by vans. I didn't know everyone. Mem said Dodde had invited people who he wanted to help lay the cellar walls. Mem came out of the house and shook hands with everyone, smiling, happier than I'd seen her since the night she fainted in the kitchen doorway. After all the handshakes, Uncle Dan said, "Well, uhh, we better get to work; we've got a cellar to lay."

"Okay, boys," Dodde said. "Let's get that cement mixed up. We'll need some water. And the wheelbarrow and an old hoe."

As the men set to work, Mem said to Marie and Maudie, "Lomie and Lizzie are in the garden. Would you like to go help them pick corn?"

Lizzie and I waved, pretending we'd just come to the edge of the field. Marie and Maudie walked down to where we were.

"Want to help?" Lizzie asked, holding out one handle of the basket to Marie, who took it. Maudie and I followed them back into the cornfield.

"Let's husk these outside," Aunt Saloma said when we brought the basket filled with corn to the house. She and the other aunts took the basket out to the benches in the shade and sat down to husk and visit.

Maudie, Marie, Lizzie, and I ran to the cellar hole and stood with the other children as close as we could get and still be out of the way. Dodde poured fine gray powder from a large bag into the wheelbarrow and added water from the pail Joe and Cousin Andy brought from the pump. Datt stirred it with a hoe. I watched as the gray powder turned into thick mud.

"Lizzie! Lomie!" Mem called from the kitchen door. She held Baby Simon. As we came up to her, she said, "Lizzie, take him to Aunt Sarah and see if she will hold him. If he cries, bring him to me. Lomie, we need some potatoes from the cellar. And then you both can set up the small bathtub with some soap and towels in the yard for the men to wash in, out near the church benches."

The morning went by quickly. I watched Datt and several other men carrying the cement blocks. Dodde directed the laying of the blocks for the walls, which got higher one layer at a time. The men joked about who was strongest and who worked the hardest.

Around noon, the food was all set out. Besides Mem's chicken, mashed potatoes and gravy, and fresh ears of corn, there was Aunt Ada's baked beans, Momme's homemade bread that tasted just like Mem's, and tomatoes and beans from the garden. For dessert there would be cake, pudding, and ground-cherry pies. I hoped the men would leave some for the women and girls.

The men washed up, and then everyone bowed their heads for *Händt nunna*. After a long moment, Dodde cleared his throat, and then everyone moved. I looked at him in surprise. This was Datt's home, so wasn't it his place to end the "Hands down"? I wondered. But Datt was already moving into the line of men to fill their plates, and I couldn't see his expression.

After the men had taken their plates to the church benches and eaten, the boys sitting with their full plates on the ground around them, the women and girls could go to the table and fill their plates. I sat down on the ground beside Lizzie, Marie, and Maudie. I tried not to eat too fast, but it was hard, because the food was so good. When I was done, I had that nice, full, satisfied feeling that the Amish called *sot*. This was a word that described it so much better than the English word, "full." One could be full but not satisfied. *Sot* said it all in one short word, and that is exactly what I felt after the frolic meal. While the aunts did the dishes, Lizzie pushed the girl cousins on the swing. She could push so that the tall swing would go far and fast. When it was my turn and she pushed me, I was swinging higher than the roof on the woodshed, with the wind rushing past my ears and excitement tickling my stomach. I could see Mem and the aunts moving around in the house propped above the cellar hole. Their voices echoed as they chatted about the work that needed to be done. All of sudden, they screamed and made for the door with their aprons over their heads, trying to get down the shaky, bendy planks. What looked like a black bird flew out of one of the broken windowpanes. They had startled a bat, and the bat startled them. They stood around outside, laughing and daring one another to go back in. Most of the women wouldn't go back in, because they were afraid that there would be more bats. I asked, "Why did they put their aprons over their heads?"

"So the bat wouldn't get tangled in their hair," Lizzie said.

I wondered how a bat could possibly get caught in the women's hair—each one of them had her hair tied up into a bun and was wearing a *kop*. Lizzie said, "Lomie, it's someone else's turn now." I got off the swing and Maudie took her turn.

Finally, just as it started to get dark, the walls reached the same height as the cellar under the house. They were taller than Uncle Dan, and he was the tallest uncle. The following week, after the walls had had time to set, Dodde and a few close neighbors would come back and lower the house down onto them. The work of the frolic was finished. Everybody began leaving, tired, but I saw men nodding when they looked back. I watched them go and thought about how it must feel to build something all day, and then be able to look at it, all done, at sunset.

MEM'S HARD WORK on the house was yet to come. For the rest of the fall, she spent every free moment she had working in the old house. At first, when I came home from school there would be piles of old plaster waiting to be taken to the trash pile back in the woods. When all the old plaster was gone, Mem mixed up new plaster and smoothed it over the lath walls and ceiling, and when that had dried, she put on another layer. She took out the light switches and filled in the holes. When she finished putting up new wallpaper, it began to look more like a house.

Dodde came and put in new windows and made a doorway between the two houses on the first floor and in the upstairs. Now we didn't have two separate houses, but one big one. Mem painted the woodwork, and finally cleaned the floor and painted it gray. We washed the windows, and when Mem hung clean new curtains and laid woven rugs on the floor, it began to feel like part of our very own house. We moved in as we were getting our first snow.

Even though we had more room in our house, it did not change Mem's level of responsibilities. She was just as stressed and worked as hard as always.

MY WEEKS AT SMITH were both short and long—they were short because I enjoyed my studies and there was always something fun to do, but they were long in missing David. Therefore, I looked forward to packing up my laundry and books and heading for home after my German class on Friday afternoons. On this Friday afternoon, the three hours went by quickly as I listened to German tapes along the way. I arrived home and saw David moving about in the kitchen. He saw me coming and came out to help me carry my belongings in. We hugged out by the driveway. David held back, and I said, "You haven't seen me all week and you aren't giving me a real hug?"

"Let's go in where it's private," David said with a smile playing at the corners of his mouth. I looked across the top of the car at him and laughed. "You always did have to have absolute privacy for a simple hug and a kiss. Fine, then—you are going to get it when we get in the house."

"No, *you* are going to get it," he laughed.

It was worth the privacy to wait for David's hugs and kisses. I saw him as if he were new to me. He was so handsome—fair, clear skin, a high forehead, and full red lips. His hair is barely streaked with gray, even though he is almost fifty, and I love his blue, blue eyes that are so expressive. I can often tell his mood by reading his eyes. At this moment, I could tell his mood was the same as mine. Our passion came first, our dinner second.

After dinner, I started my laundry. David and I settled down for a movie. We sat next to one another on the couch, our bodies hungry for the touch we had missed all week.

When we were snuggled into bed for the night, I said, "I have been having vivid memories of Datt every night this week as I went to sleep."

"What kinds of memories?"

"Mostly I remembered the times when I was really little and frightened by his state of mind. Those times seem so dark to me now. It seems to me he brought sorrow to so many people's lives, and his own life was so filled with sorrow. I just have to ask, what is the meaning of such a life?"

"I don't know," David said. "Maybe it is one of those mysteries that we will never know the answer to."

"It just seems that it is an unfair lot that Datt never experienced real joy in his life."

"How do you know that he didn't? Maybe he experienced joy in smaller ways than most people. What about the time he got his job at the orchard?"

"You could be right. I have never seen him so happy before or since." With my head on David's chest, I remembered.

I was about seven years old. Datt had been without a job, and Mem often prodded him off his rocking chair and urged him to go and look for one. Late one afternoon, after Datt had been away for most of the day, he suddenly came bounding up the driveway, yelling and clapping his hands above his head and shouting, "*Ich happ en cha-ap! Ich happ en cha-ap! Ich happ en cha-ap!*" (I have a jo-ob . . .). I had never seen him so exuberant.

Mem looked out and saw what Datt was doing, and a smile crossed her face. She said, "Well, what has gotten into *him?*"

Datt came in and told us. In the fall he would be picking peaches, apples, and pears at an orchard, and in the spring he would prune the fruit trees. He would be working with other Amish men at the orchard.

Datt's happiest days were when he was working in the orchard. He seemed to have one area of intelligence—trees. When I walked through the woods with him in the spring, tapping maples, he would be able to name every kind of tree on his forty acres. Each of the trees seemed like one of his friends. I often felt that he cared more for his trees than for his family. Now, as I reflected on this, I was just glad that he had a passion in his life. I wonder if part of Datt's depression was because of his feelings of inadequacy in the community. There was basically one role for an Amish married man to play—to provide for his family. If Datt felt like a failure in this role, he might have felt like he couldn't do anything worthwhile.

David's breathing got deeper, and I knew he had fallen asleep. I kept my head on his chest, and breathed in his smell, and listened to the snores deep in his chest. I was so grateful for his support. It is staggering to read the statistics for how many women who grow up in abusive families end up finding partners who are like their abusers. David is so different from either Datt or Joe. All couples have difficulties, but we have a base of love and support for one another that carries us through these difficulties. I thought about what one of my housemates had told me—that the odds of Ada Comstock scholars coming to Smith married and leaving divorced were high. I hoped David's and my relationship was not going to add to these numbers.

Do You Remember Me?

Back at Smith, my struggles to stay focused grew more intense. As I awoke in my window bed one morning, I realized that my days belonged to Smith, and my nights belonged to my memories—though there were times when my memories intruded while I was sitting in class. Most of the time I could keep the two separate, but with each passing day, as Datt kept failing, it became increasingly harder to concentrate on my studies.

Just as I was deciding I might regret not going back to see Datt for the last time, an email arrived from Sister Susan, reporting that Datt's struggle with life had ended at around 2:00 that afternoon, with family members around him.

When I called David to tell him of Datt's death, he was sympathetic and supportive. But when I told him I felt we should set out for Ohio the next morning, he balked. The trustees at the museum where he worked were coming to see an exhibit he had been working on for two years—he insisted we could not leave until he had walked them through the building. It would take him until noon, putting us in Ohio around midnight.

"Where are we going to stay?" David asked.

"I don't know. If we are coming in that late, it is not appropriate to ask anyone in my family."

"How about we stay with my sister?"

"That would be nice, actually. It would give us a reprieve from the Amish and the intensity of what's happening in my own family. But Bernadette and Maurice go to bed so early."

"Yeah, but maybe they could leave the door open for us."

"Do you mind calling them?"

"I can do that."

"Okay, good. What are we going to do about Tim? He's on break from school this week, isn't he?"

"Yes. He will have to come with us."

"Can you have him pack his clothes, and make sure he has the appropriate clothes with dark pants, dark jacket, and a white shirt?"

"Sure. What about a tie?"

"You would probably both be better off without ties for an Amish funeral, but that is up to you," I said. "But what are we going to do about the fact that you are in Vermont and I am in Massachusetts?"

"I will just have to come down and get you tomorrow."

"I think it would be better for me to drive up there tonight to save ourselves a few hours tomorrow."

"That's up to you."

"Okay, I'd better get on the road. Don't forget to call Bernadette."

TIM AND I HAD THE CAR packed when David got home a bit before noon. We ate a quick lunch and began our journey west, across the bridge over Lake Champlain to New York State. The autumn colors were beginning to show on the mountains, and the lake was a sparkling blue. We curved in and around the Adirondacks to the New York State Thruway. Tim had brought his earphones and was listening to music in the back seat. David and I talked about how this time away might affect my first semester at Smith, and we also talked about the world I was about to reenter after leaving it twenty-four years before.

We drove through Amsterdam, then got on Interstate 90 to travel another four hundred miles to Ohio. David talked about the route that had been familiar to him since his childhood, when his family used to visit his grandparents in Cleveland from his family's home, first in New York State, and then later Vermont. As we drove past the Indian Castle rest stop, David recalled once more the night they were stranded there in a snowstorm, when the interstate was closed down. His mother had multiple sclerosis, and she used to get immobilized by the cold. She wrapped herself in blankets that they got at the rest stop, and his father kept running the car off and on. The rest stop served hot drinks all night for free. Somehow they made it through the night, and the next day they continued on their way.

We stopped along the way to change drivers. I drove the middle stint, past the bird sanctuary in Montezuma, while David slept and Tim listened to music. I tried remembering the last time my whole family had been together in one place, and I realized I didn't know when that was. Even Datt's death was not going to bring everyone together. I felt sorry for Sister Katherine. She lives in a group home in Kentucky because she is mentally challenged and cannot be independent. Sister Susan and I had tried to secure a ride for her to Ohio from Kentucky, but her caregivers were uncooperative. We didn't know what communications had taken place between Joe and the home where Katherine lived, and in the end Susan and I had to accept that it was out of our hands.

Lizzie would also not be there. She had visited Datt the week before, when he was dying, and said she could not afford to come back again. Perhaps it was for the best, because her previous visit to Ohio had been stressful for both Sarah and Susan, who put her up as well as her daughter, Audrey. Sarah had warned Lizzie to keep her medications well out of reach of Sarah's little children, but one morning when she came into the kitchen, her three-year-old was holding a bottle of Lizzie's pills that would have been harmful had she consumed any.

To make matters worse, Lizzie totaled her car while she was in Ohio, then tried to use that as an excuse to linger. Susan helped her to acquire a plane ticket and told Lizzie she could not stay with her any longer. Family dynamics such as these were set in motion long ago in our childhood. Lizzie was seen as the black sheep of the family, and now played the victim role to perfection.

Very early on, Mem handed the eldest-daughter role to me, making Lizzie feel even more inadequate. It didn't help that I showed off how much smarter I thought I was. When Lizzie was in seventh grade, Mem would grill her on her times tables every night as she set the table. To show that I knew them better than she did, I would answer for her. If I had been the mother in that situation, I would have told "Lomie" in no uncertain terms to be quiet. What I didn't realize at the time is that I was playing the role that Mem expected me to. She didn't mind making Lizzie feel inferior. It was as if she wanted to "remake" Lizzie, rather than accepting her with all her shortcomings.

Lizzie could turn her temper onto any one of us younger siblings without warning. Her normal method of violence was to make a fist and hit us with the bottom of both hands, as if her arms were a threshing machine and her hands were hammers. My inclination was to turn my back to her to protect my face, and so she would beat my back full force with both her arms, her hands landing on my back, hard and fast like hammers, over and over. When I got older, I fought back, but it was like a fight between a beagle dog and a boxer—I didn't stand a chance.

We sisters had to share beds when we were growing up. We all hated to share a bed with Lizzie, because she thrashed about throughout the night. Once in the middle of the night, she lashed out in her dream of fighting someone, and I got the back of her hand smack in my face, full force. When I suddenly awoke and cried because it hurt so badly, she kept repeating that she was sleeping and didn't do it intentionally. I told her it still hurt, whether it was intentional or not, which she didn't seem to understand.

There was one time in my life when I got along well with Lizzie. It was the fall I was fourteen and she was sixteen. When Datt first mentioned that she and I could get a job at the orchard, picking up drops, I didn't exactly look forward to working in the same place as Datt—until I got to the orchard. It was one of the most beautiful places I had ever seen. The trees, laden with apples, were planted in rows, and around the edges of the orchard were woods. Some of the woods were pine trees planted in straight rows, and then there were tall walnut trees, as well as the usual beech, hickory, maple, elm, and oak trees I recognized from our own woods. The oak trees at the orchard were bigger than any I'd ever seen.

Lizzie and I sorted the apples under the tree, throwing the rotten ones towards the tree trunk and picking the good ones into wooden crates. We got paid ten cents a bushel. I loved the cool autumn air, and we ate all the crisp, sweet apples we wanted. We'd have a picnic at lunchtime, sitting on crates. We hardly ever saw anyone except one another. I don't remember having any disagreements with Lizzie during our time at the orchard, except for the day I got both of us in trouble. On this day, we were working close to a ravine. We looked down and saw a brook running through the ravine, with a wooden footbridge over it. Tall trees shaded the area, and there was a picnic table near the brook. There was a carpet of newly fallen leaves of red, orange, and gold under the tall trees. All morning, as we sorted and picked up apples, I tried to convince Lizzie that it wouldn't hurt to go down there to the picnic table to eat our lunch. She kept saying, "But we don't have permission. What if we get into trouble?" When lunchtime came, I convinced her it was okay to at least take a walk. We walked down the path, through a grove of pine trees. She kept saying, "What if we aren't supposed to do this?" I kept saying, "What's wrong with taking a walk?" At the end of the rows of pines, the trail dropped down into the ravine. As I walked through the freshly fallen leaves, I felt as though I had been in this place before. I was heading for the footbridge over the stream that reminded me of the fairy tale *Snow White and the Seven Dwarfs*, when my wonderment was suddenly interrupted by Datt's angry and frantic voice booming down into the ravine. He yelled loudly, "Lomie! Lizzie! Where are you?"

"Right here!" I called back.

"You girls get back up here right now!"

"Okay!" I called.

"I told you we shouldn't have done this," Lizzie said in a scared voice, all the way up the path. She was struggling to stay up with me, and she was panting. She had been obese even as a child, and at sixteen, her weight hampered her movements. By the time we got to the pine grove, Datt was already there. To cover the distance in the time he did it, I knew he must have been running. I couldn't understand why he was so upset. I told him we were going for a walk during our lunchtime, but he didn't answer—he just walked behind me at such a fast pace I felt as though he would walk into me if I didn't walk fast enough. Lizzie panted next to me, but she didn't slow down. When we got back to the spot where our crates were, Datt said, "Now you girls get to work, and you *stay* doing your work!" With that, he stomped off, each step an exclamation point to what he had just said.

We worked in a subdued way for the rest of the day. Datt didn't tell us why he was so upset. I wondered if it was only because we had left our work, or if he actually was concerned for our safety. The latter would have suggested he had paternal feelings for us, and I didn't think he was capable of that. Since this was the first time we had ever left the trees where we were sorting drops, we wondered if Datt had been keeping an eye on us all along and we didn't know it.

Our crisp autumn days at the orchard came to an end when the apples were all picked. My dream of finding that enchanted fairy-tale place in the woods where I imagined sitting by the little arched bridge for hours, watching birds and the little creatures of the forest, was never realized.

DAVID AWOKE AND OFFERED to drive again. I was happy to let him. I slept until we arrived at Bernadette and Maurice's house a bit before midnight. Bernadette had left the door open for us. We slipped in with our luggage and locked the door behind us, then found our respective bedrooms and retired for the night.

In the morning, we ate breakfast with Bernadette and Maurice. Tim was wearing a T-shirt that had a big black image showing through his dress shirt. I asked him if he had brought any other T-shirts, and he said this was fine. David chimed in and agreed with Tim and wouldn't answer me when I asked if he had brought any extras. Bernadette didn't say anything, but after breakfast she laid a white T-shirt on the chair next to Tim and told him he could borrow it if he wanted to. I didn't say anything, and Tim changed the shirt. I was grateful to Bernadette that she had prevented a power struggle. Attending Datt's wake was tense enough.

We left our car parked out at the end of the driveway and walked into the house in which I had grown up. It looked very different now: Instead of the old weathered barn of my childhood, there was now a circular driveway in front of the house, with a shop, buggy shed, and barn, and a long, low building that my brother used to house his masonry tools in the courtyard. Set back, next to this tool shed, was the little *Dodde* house Mem and Datt had lived in for the last two decades.

The entrance of the house had also changed. The stairs going up into the kitchen were in the same place they had been in my childhood, but the entrance had been built where a little outside porch had been before. The house was quiet when we went up the stairs, which I found strange. Normally the Amish have an ongoing wake from the time a person dies until after the funeral.

Joe and Emma had put in new cupboards some years ago, which updated their kitchen to look like other Amish kitchens. The floors were clean and shiny hardwood. Rows of benches stood in the kitchen and living room, but all of them were empty. One man sat by himself in the corner of the living room. "Jake Miller, married to Irene," I thought to myself. "I wonder why he's all by himself?" Jake was perhaps the least respected member in the community.

Jake asked if I remembered him, and I said I did. I wondered how I could possibly have forgotten him. He was often described in the community as "not as smart as I should be," which is the Amish way of humbling oneself while putting down someone else at the same time. Jake's wife, Irene, was known among the Amish as *schloppich* (sloppy). Together they had trouble caring for their growing family when I was a teenager. As was the custom in such a situation, other members of the Amish community took it upon themselves to help Jake and Irene. That job seemed to fall on our family. Perhaps Mem thought we could improve our own image in the community, or perhaps she just decided she had so many daughters she didn't know what to do, so she sent us to help the little woman who had so many children she didn't know what to do. My sisters and I occasionally walked the two miles to their house to clean or cook or look after their children for a day.

Jake and Irene lived in a crowded little dark part of his parents' house, and every time we went over there, we had to scrape and wash dishes that had dried-out food all over them, and then pick up the toys from the filthy floor so we could sweep and mop. A week later, when we went back, it looked like no one had washed dishes or swept the floor since the last time we had done it. Jake and Irene's situation was the only one I knew of in the community that was worse than our own. I am not certain why Jake and Irene were being helped and our family wasn't. Perhaps it was because Jake and Irene's children didn't have even one responsible parent, and we at least had Mem.

IRENE OFTEN HAD TWO or three children in diapers, but her treatment of the diapers was so negligent it was considered a health hazard. Her house usually smelled so strongly that it was obvious she let diapers go for weeks before washing any. To eliminate the problem, people in the community bought her disposable diapers. Irene then burned the dirty diapers in her woodstove. In the summer, when the stove was not going, she would let them collect in there until she decided she had had enough, and then the whole neighborhood smelled of the horrible stink that came from her chimney.

Irene was not a good cook, so quite frequently in the summer, Jake would take the little red wagon and walk the mile to the nearest town to buy several gallons of ice cream. That would be their dinner. Because the Amish don't own freezers, leftover ice cream normally is given to the neighbors—but Jake had a different idea. He would leave it out overnight, and the next morning he would slurp the melted ice cream and call it his milkshake.

JAKE SPOKE AND BROUGHT me back to the present. "The others are out in the shed eating. The patient is in the bedroom, if you want to go on in."

I found it eerie that Jake called Datt a patient: it gave me the feeling that I was about to open the bedroom door and find Datt was still alive. But I calmed the eerie feeling by telling myself that Jake had made an honest mistake.

David, Tim, and I entered the bedroom. There was Datt's body, dressed in his Sunday best, laid out on a stretcher, his still hands crossed. A window was open, with a breeze blowing through his gray beard. It gave the illusion of movement. Tim became restless after a few moments, so David left with him, leaving me alone with Datt. As if to intensify my apprehensive feelings, the door above the stairs, which had been ajar, suddenly blew shut with a decided bang. I closed the window to stop the breeze from blowing through Datt's beard, and then all was quiet. In my thoughts I told Datt that I was glad he had a peaceful death. I told him I loved him, and that I had forgiven him for his failings, and that I hoped he would find peace in the afterlife.

David opened the door and came in. He put his arm around me, and then the tears came. I looked at David and said, "No matter what, it is still the end of a life. There is sadness in that alone. And he was my father, after all." David took a tissue from the box on a stand in the corner of the room and gave it to me. We heard people coming into the house. I said, "We should probably go out." I put my hand on Datt's and looked at him again. He looked as if he had just fallen asleep.

When I stepped into the living room, I saw my cousin Mary; my sisters-in-law, Emma and Linda; and many other church women. I shook hands with all of them, and the ones I hadn't seen since I'd left asked, *"Meinst mich noch?"* (Do you remember me?) as they shook my hand. The people I remembered grinned broadly, and the ones I didn't remember seemed disappointed.

Mem came in and hobbled over with her three-pronged cane to sit in a rocking chair in the corner of the living room. Her hands and arms were arthritic, looking like gnarly tree branches. She dropped her large frame into the bent hickory rocker. David has often likened Mem's physical presence to that of a mourning dove, with a large body and a small head. She looked tired and sad. Normally her face looked younger, with her light blue eyes and fair skin that was far less wrinkled than most women at eighty-three, but two days after Datt's death she looked her age. David, Tim, and I sat with her. I asked her how she was doing, and she said pretty good. She said, "I am so glad he isn't suffering any more. But oh, Saloma, it was so hard when he died. I just thought I *had* to help him." Susan had told me that Dad had aspirated in his last moments and that Mem had focused on trying to wipe it away until Joe had caught her arm and said, "Mem, let it go." It was as if Mem had been trying to wipe away death itself—her own form of denial at the very end.

I said to Mem, "I heard about that. Do you know that having that kind of thing happen at the end is quite common? That happened with David's Mom. One of his sisters said Ruth looked as if she was drowning."

Mem's face got red with emotion. I said, "Mem, you have to know that you did everything you could for him. Not just at the last minute, but for the last fifty years."

Mem's tears spilled down her cheeks. I held her hand and cried with her. "I know you are going to miss him," I said.

"Oh, but I am just so glad he is in a better place," Mem said. She cried until her tears were spent.

Brother Simon came over and heartily shook my hand. It felt like his hand was twice as big as mine. He said, "I read your letters to Mom and Dad." He had tears in his eyes as he said, "I was so touched." To my surprise, here was my younger brother, who was physically big and strong, moved to tears over the letters I had written.

"So you read them?"

"Yes, I did. The way you can write is such a gift!"

"Why, thank you, Simon." I was still reeling with the knowledge that Mem had shared the letters, which I had intended to be private.

Later, Mem said something about her sisters reading the letters, and I asked, "So you let other people read those letters?"

"I didn't exactly. They snooped and read them. They were lying on my dresser."

"Nosy them," I said.

"Yes," Mem said with wan smile. Then she added, "I hope you don't mind, but I shared them with other people too."

"I noticed. Simon mentioned that he'd read them. I thought they were going to be private, but I guess if you don't have a problem sharing them, I don't either." I gulped down my disappointment, knowing that at this point it wouldn't matter even if I did mind. I couldn't take away the fact that Mem had already shared them.

The afternoon passed quickly as people came and went. I had very little time to talk with David and Tim as I continued to visit with many people.

The Amish people began filing out to Joe's shop for supper. Joe's workshop had been built adjacent to a buggy shed, on the site where our old chicken coop used to stand. It was big enough to set up tables and benches for a large group of people. I could imagine the beehive of women out there, preparing food and serving people as they came in. David nudged me and suggested we go to the local restaurant that serves Amish-style food. I agreed. No one had invited us to come out with them, and I wasn't sure whether they were set up for us to eat separately from the others. Because I had left the community, they shunned me, which meant they couldn't eat with me, accept gifts from me, ride in cars driven by me, or do business with me.

The enforcement of these rules is a bit arbitrary in my home community. It often depends on what church district one lives in, and sometimes which family within the district, as to how strictly one enforces the shunning. At first after I left the community, when David and I went back to visit, my mother had us eat right with the family, but then she was criticized for that. The next time we visited, she set a separate table for us, but it was only a few inches away from the family table. She was criticized for that, too, so then she stopped eating with us altogether. She still accepted gifts on the sly, and on several occasions she rode in the car with David and me.

The minute we were in the car, Tim starting firing questions at me. "Mom, if you have so many first cousins, how many second cousins do I have?"

"Too many to count," I said. "Think of yourself as Rabbit in *Winnie the Pooh*, as in Rabbit's friends and relations."

Tim laughed. "Now, Mom, that's funny. You don't usually say funny things, but that's actually pretty funny. But do you know how many first cousins you have?"

"I have 96 on Mom's side of the family, and if I remember correctly, there are 76 on Dad's side."

"So you have like 172 first cousins? Oh my God! Mom, are you some kind of celebrity with these people, even though you left?"

"I wouldn't say that, but I have to say I am surprised by the reception I'm getting. I had no idea people would be this friendly."

"How long has it been since you've seen these people?"

"I've not seen most of them since I left the second time, which was twenty-four years ago."

"Do you still remember them?"

"Oh, Tim, don't ask me that. *Everyone* is asking me that question. And they seem really disappointed when I don't remember them. Did you see that man with the long, dark beard I was talking to?"

"You mean the man sitting in the middle of the living room?"

"Yes. He was a fourth-grade student when I taught school. He is now a father of several children, and he asked me that same question."

Tim chuckled. "That's pretty funny. Did he really expect you to remember him?"

"I don't know. Oh, Tim, I have to tell you something funny. My sister-in-law, Emma, asked me if your curls are natural."

"What?"

"Tim, you do have unusual hair, whether it's inside or outside the Amish."

"But why did she ask that?"

"She said my cousin Mary had asked her that. Her son, Nevin, apparently has hair just like yours."

"One of my relations, you mean?"

"Yes," I laughed. "That kind of curly hair comes from my grandfather on my mother's side of the family."

"Really?"

"Yes, but more often than not, it's red and curly."

"I saw some people with hair so red, it was almost orange," Tim said.

"Yup, that's it."

"Thank God I don't have hair that color."

"I rather like it, actually."

"Mom, you're kidding me!"

"No, I'm not. I felt cheated as a young girl that I didn't end up with red hair. Of all Mom's siblings who married and had children, she was the only one who didn't have any children with red hair."

"Your brother Simon has a red beard, though."

"Oh, yes, you're right."

David said, "Tim, you fit right in with your long hair. It's just about as long as an Amish man's."

I looked at Tim across the table and realized that my gorgeous child had grown into a handsome young man. His eyes are as blue as David's; his skin is fair, like both David's and mine; and he has fine features, including a characteristic pug nose, also from Mem's side of the family.

Tim had been a handful ever since he was young child. Now he was testing David's and my limits in all the ways teenagers do, such as smoking marijuana and rebelling against our rules. While I often wanted to hold him responsible for his behavior, David preferred to be Tim's friend instead of parent and enforcer. Our different parenting styles were the main source of our disagreements. Now I saw a different side of Tim, as I watched his keen interest in various aspects of the Amish culture. The depth of his questions concerning his heritage surprised me.

WHEN WE STEPPED INTO the entrance at Joe's house, someone came forward and shook my hand and asked the stock question, *"Meinst mich noch?"* that many others had asked before him.

"Of course," I answered. "You are Rube's Dave. You are the funeral director. And I remember that I used to come and visit you and Katie when I was a teacher at Meadow Glow School."

He had a twinkle in his eye that I could see even in the semidarkness of the entrance. He kept holding onto my hand and looking me in the eye, as if to say, "We understand one another."

When we opened the door, the kitchen was filled with people sitting on rows of backless benches. I started shaking hands, but then realized it would take too long to shake everyone's hand, and walked into the living room, where I sat next to Susan and her husband, Bill. Lines of people came by and shook hands with us family members, then went into the bedroom to pay their respects to my father. They exited through the other bedroom door and sat in the kitchen or living room and visited.

In between lines of people shaking hands, Susan and I visited. Susan is the smallest of all the women in my family. She works hard at not having the "Mose Miller" figure. (My maternal great-grandfather was short and stout, and most of the relatives on Mem's side of the family blame their girth on this branch of the family.) If you lined up the women cousins and aunts on Mem's side of the family and covered their faces, it would be hard to tell one person from another, with their wide hips and protruding stomachs. Except for a few cousins and Susan. She is short and pretty, and because of scoliosis and her own vow to not let herself go, she has carefully controlled her weight. She cleans houses professionally and exercises daily. With her gray-green eyes and full red lips, many would call her beautiful—except for a lingering unhappiness that shows in her face. She and her husband, Bill, have struggled in their marriage for many years. They became born-again Christians and left the Amish many years ago. They are raising five children, ranging in age from six to twenty-two.

A whole group of Datt's relatives came through the living room. They had just arrived by chartered bus. David watched the line of people move through, shaking hands as they went, then suggested we move outside to make more space. It had gotten dark, and one of the aunts from Wisconsin was walking in the driveway with a flashlight. Tim pointed and said, "Wait a minute, how is it that they can use flashlights? That's using electricity!" My first reaction was to say it wasn't electricity, but then I realized Tim was right and that he was looking at it from an outsider's point of view. I had never questioned why we were allowed to use flashlights, even though we couldn't have electricity. David explained to Tim that by staying off the grid, the Amish were able to pick and choose which technologies they would allow, but if they had electricity coming into the houses, then they could no longer prevent people from having anything they wanted.

A few minutes later, a buggy rushed past us and out the lane. Tim pointed and said, "What, they have LED lights on that buggy!"

"Well, Tim, that is a new one on me, too. LEDs were not yet invented by the time I left the community. I am surprised they allow them myself."

David whispered to me, "That group that just came through looked like they just stepped out of the Civil War era."

"Yeah, they are from Wisconsin, one of the strictest Amish communities I know of. Did you see the size of the men's hat brims and how deep the women's bonnets are?"

"No, but the men's hands are all so big, mine got lost in theirs when I shook hands. I feel like I just stepped back in time, seeing these people."

"Now you know what I feel like," I said.

Susan and Bill joined us outside. Bill looked ill at ease. In his heart and mind, Bill is still Amish, but because he isn't part of the community any longer, he is out of his element. Susan told us that we were expected to be there the next morning at eight o'clock, an hour before the service was to begin, and that we would line up to go into the service according to age. We both were surprised at this—we would have thought that the Amish segment of the family would go in first.

MAURICE MET US AT THE door when we arrived at his and Bernadette's house. He opened the door, then said, "David and Tim can come in," and closed the door again.

I said, "Come on, Maurice, you should be nice to me tonight."

"Why is that?" he asked.

"Because my father died," I said.

"Oh, okay," he said, and opened the door with a sheepish smile. He had greeted me in his usual fashion. We had been teasing one another for many years. David usually joined in, and Bernadette would laugh at all of it. Sometimes Maurice and I would turn our duel of wits into a cutthroat Scrabble game.

Bernadette offered us wine, and we sat on the comfortable chairs in their living room. She wanted to know all about what was happening. Talking about it helped us unwind from the day. When we were relaxed and the four of us were in a round of yawning, Bernadette, David, and Maurice retired for the night.

Tim had many more questions, and he and I stayed up for another hour, as I tried to answer his questions the best way I could.

When he asked why they had rules about plain clothes, I explained that from the Amish point of view, fancy clothes promote pride in the individual, and that the Amish stress the importance of community more than individuality.

"But we are all individuals." Tim said.

"But when you think about how we define individuality in mainstream American culture—as having independence and personal freedom—it is the opposite in the Amish community. Their definition of a strong individual is one who blends into the community well. Our idea of blending feels like annihilation of individuality, but the Amish see blending as a virtue and a sign of a strong person."

"That's strange. But why do the Amish not believe in technology?"

"There has always been a strong emphasis on hard work and connection to the earth in the Amish culture, and most technologies are seen as distracting from that emphasis. But you know, the Amish do allow certain technologies. Sometimes it seems like there is no rhyme or reason to these decisions, but that often has to do with who was in charge when the discussion of a particular kind of technology came up. An example of that is when chain saws first became available. My grandfather was advocating for the use of chain saws, but there were others who opposed it. The Amish in my home community allowed chain saws, but I don't know whether all Amish communities allow them or not."

"So it's arbitrary?"

"Yes." Then I added, "The Amish set of church rules are both arbitrary and absolute."

"But isn't that a contradiction?" Tim asked.

"You could look at it that way. But, someone can make an arbitrary rule and then be absolute about people obeying the rule, whether it makes sense or not."

"So are most of their rules based on the Anabaptist rules from Europe, like back in the 1600s?"

"Yes, but when new technologies come into being, they have to deal with each one, which is something their forefathers didn't need to deal with," I said.

"But isn't that the same problem that other fundamentalist religions have? They are trying to live by the rules made in a different time and place, whether or not they are applicable?"

"Yes. Not only are they not taking into account that times have changed, but they are *denying* that they have changed, which sometimes makes their way of life so restrictive that it becomes punitive. Much focus is put on punishing wrongdoers, as opposed to finding harmony in the community."

"But, the community sure works well together. Look at the way everyone is working together for your Dad's wake and funeral," Tim said.

"Absolutely. That is partly because everyone has a fixed place in the community. When people accept their place in the community, a lot can be accomplished. That is something the rest of the world could learn from the

Amish. But most of us are not willing to make the sacrifices that it takes to be a part of such a community."

"I sure wouldn't!"

"Really?"

"Mom! Don't you know me better than that? You were a rebel, too. You ought to understand why I wouldn't have done well here in the community."

"I also think you might have done better with a close-knit community. You seem to need more structure in your life than you have."

"I need to get to bed," Tim said, suddenly shifting the focus.

"Yes, me too," I said, yawning.

David was already asleep as I settled into bed. Sleep was slow in coming. I remembered how Datt was happiest during sugaring season. Then my thoughts went back to the year I was ten.

One afternoon in February when we came home from school, Mem was working in the basement in a cloud of steam. She had heated water in the big iron pot for washing sap buckets. The iron pot sat on a steel jacket that had a door where we could build a fire under the pot, and a stovepipe connected this jacket to the chimney. We called the whole thing a cooker, which we used to heat water for washing clothes, and for washing sap buckets once a year.

Mem asked us to change our clothes. Usually we dragged out that part. We dreaded doing the work around the house on a typical day. My sisters and I called it drudgery. But, on this day we did it quickly because we liked washing sap buckets.

The tops of the stacks of buckets were lost in a cloud of steam when I got to the basement. I asked Datt how many there were and he said more than nine hundred.

Datt separated the buckets. When two of them stuck together, he held them in one hand and tapped the rim of the bottom bucket with a hammer until they came apart. Lizzie, Sarah, and I took turns washing and rinsing. Susan was the youngest, so she carried the buckets to whoever was stacking them in the newer part of the basement. My favorite part was stacking. I liked building the pyramids in rows all along the cellar wall by lining up the buckets upside down on the floor, then placing the next row of buckets on top of that, resting one bucket on top of two underneath. I'd build each pyramid as high as the ceiling, then another one in front of the first one.

As I counted and stacked, I heard Datt's tap, tap, tapping on the bucket rims, then the hollow bang as the bucket hit the cement floor. I heard the grating of the buckets against the cast iron tub and the swish, swishing of Lizzie's brush. I hummed a tune, and the sound vibrated around the rims of the buckets. I left room for a path through the middle of the basement and filled up the rest with pyramids.

"Only one more row," I said to Datt when I came to carry more buckets.

"How many are there so far?" he asked.

"Four hundred and seventy," I said.

When the last row was stacked, we emptied the tubs, and then we swept the water toward the drain in the floor. Datt and Lizzie went upstairs.

Sarah, Susan, and I stood in the path between the pyramids and called out vowel sounds, then listened to the sounds bounce around each bucket rim in turn, before it faded into nowhere. We called out "OOOO, EEEE, AAAA!" and waited for the echo.

Sarah and Susan soon tired of playing the echo game and went upstairs. I listened to my echo by myself, and then I sat on the basement steps and looked at the faint light coming through the little windows over the tops of the pyramids. I thought of all the other years when we had created an echo chamber with the sap buckets. I felt as though I was a little girl again, even though I was ten. I wondered if in another year I would think I was too old, as Lizzie had this time.

I was sitting in the dark when I got a whiff of Mem's supper and I suddenly realized I was famished. I took off my boots at the landing. When I walked into the kitchen, I blinked in the light of the lantern. Mem was pulling baked beans out of the oven, with rows of sizzling bacon on top. She placed the pan on hot pads in the middle of the table with steaming slices of bread and a big bowl of applesauce.

After the dishes were done and the floor swept, and everyone was reading, sewing, or playing games, I felt content.

We finished washing sap buckets the next day after school. Datt scattered the clean buckets throughout the woods the following day. When we came home that afternoon, Mem said Datt was out tapping trees and he wanted us to go and help him as soon as we could. She described which part of the woods he was in. At first when we called out to him he didn't hear us. So we stayed still for a while until we heard a tap, tap, tap.

Datt had a big toothless grin when he saw us and showed us how fast the sap was running. We followed him around the woods as he drilled holes, one or two in each tree. Lizzie carried the bucket of spouts that we called spiles and stuck them into the drilled holes. I tapped them firmly with a hammer. Sarah and Susan hung the buckets and put on the covers.

Datt knew where to drill the holes. He changed where he drilled the holes each year, so the old ones could heal. He didn't hang as many buckets on each tree as other farmers; only the biggest trees got three buckets. Other farmers might have put five or six on those same trees, but Datt believed it wasn't good for the trees to put on too many. He had bought the forty acres because of the trees.

It felt good to help Datt with what he loved doing, as I tramped through the woods in the fresh spring air and watched the first sap drip out of the spiles in the maple trees.

As dusk was gathering, Datt said we would finish the next day. On our way home, from the tops of the tallest trees, we heard a bird whistle its lonesome *Wheeeee—Whooooooo!* We imitated it, and the bird answered back. Sarah said it was the chickadee's mating call. She liked studying birds and animals.

Mem had made scalloped potatoes, meatloaf, fried carrots, and applesauce with whipped cream. Everything tasted so delicious. I knew Mem would be out in the sugarhouse boiling sap in a few days, and we would make do with eating in shifts and bringing her or Datt their supper in the sugarhouse. I decided to enjoy this while it lasted.

Mem helped with the dishes, because she knew we were tired. Lizzie swept the floor, and the kitchen looked nice when we were done.

ON A SATURDAY WHEN sugaring was in full swing, I helped gather nine out of twelve tanks of sap. I walked from tree to tree, pouring the sap into a larger bucket and carrying it to the tank on the wagon pulled by our workhorses, Don and Tops. When the tank was full, Datt drove the horses, pulling the load of sap, to the hill above the sugarhouse. I knew I shouldn't talk to him when he was concentrating on getting the wagon lined up with the metal pan where he would unload the sap. He would lean to his right, hold the reins taut, and then suddenly yell, "Whoa." He would then let the pipe on the gathering tank down onto a metal pan with a pipe connected to the storage tank inside the sugarhouse. If he didn't line up the wagon right, he would have to go around in a circle with the load of sap and make another pass. He would get impatient with the horses and yell at them when that happened.

During one of Datt's trips back to the sugarhouse, I stayed in the woods. I found a stone to sit on, so I could absorb the sounds of the forest. The water from the snow and spring rains soaking into the ground sounded like bubbles popping. I could hear the cars go by out on Forest Road. I heard leaves rustling. I looked behind me and saw a rabbit. I watched it and wondered if it knew I was there. I heard the hammering of a bird and saw a redheaded woodpecker high up in one of the maples. I watched him for a long time as he flew in and around the tall branches. Chickadees, nuthatches, and tufted titmice darted in and out of a big bush with red berries on it. When they all flew away at the same time, I heard the jingle of the horses' harnesses, and I looked up the trail and saw Datt coming back. I was rested and ready to gather more sap.

Mem boiled as fast as she could, so there would be space in the storage tank for the loads coming in. I liked getting the first whiff of the boiling syrup when we got close to the sugarhouse. I walked into the warm steam with the smell all around me and heard the sap pouring into the storage tank. Mem had some warm eggs that were boiled in the sap. I ate one and then I got to taste the new syrup from a cup.

At the end of the day, the horses would get ornery. Whenever they were headed in the direction of home, they would run. Sometimes they wouldn't stay standing in one place while we were gathering. Datt would yell at them, but that only made them worse.

Sugaring was a good time of the year, I decided, as I brought Datt's supper to the sugarhouse that night. It was the time that Datt worked hard and we could get along with him. I walked around the last mud puddle and hoped that Datt was still in a good mood. I stood outside the sugarhouse door and said, "Datt, can you open up?" He did. He smiled when he saw the supper I had brought. I could tell he enjoyed the solitude of the sugarhouse after a long day of gathering sap.

"Thank you for helping me today. You did a good job," Datt said. I was so shocked, I stopped in the middle of unwrapping Datt's plate of food.

I REFLECTED ON HOW all that is left of Datt's life on this earth are the memories we have of him. I was glad I had at least a few pleasant ones. I thought about his funeral that would take place in the morning, and I realized that the plan for us to be there an hour before the service is like a recurring dream I've had ever since I left the Amish. In this dream, there is always a church service about to happen, but everyone is waiting for me to arrive before beginning the service. I cannot go there until I have my Amish clothes on, and yet my organdy cape and apron no longer fit me. I usually awake in a sweat.

Funeral Circle

Datt's funeral did not resemble my recurring dream; in fact, it was as if I had converted the dream. I did not feel uncomfortable in my "high" clothing, surrounded by the four hundred other people at Datt's funeral, most of them in Amish clothes. I didn't need to wear Amish clothing that no longer fit me—either psychologically or physically.

Rube's Dave, the man who had shaken my hand so heartily the night before, had directed the attendees of the funeral where to sit. They were seated on rows of backless benches, lined up the width of the shed. In most Amish communities, church services, weddings, and funerals are held in people's houses or in one of the outbuildings on the premises. Many of the church services of my childhood were held in the tops of barns, in the sheds where farm machinery was stored, or indoors when the weather no longer permitted outdoor services. Datt's funeral service was being held in the shed Joe had built for the purpose of storing his masonry equipment. The day was cool enough that some women had their shawls wrapped around them.

Datt's closed coffin was right inside the door, with Mem sitting in her wheelchair at the foot end of his coffin. Next to Mem sat Joe and his wife, Emma. Because Sister Lizzie had not been able to travel from Kansas, I was the next in line according to age. David sat next to me. I wondered what he was thinking about these experiences, so different from his Roman Catholic upbringing. On the other side of David sat Sister Sarah and her husband, John. Sister Susan and her husband, Bill, were next, and at the end of the bench sat Brother Simon and his wife, Linda. Sister Katherine would have been sitting next to Linda if Susan and I had been successful in getting her a ride from Kentucky. Here was the symbol for all to see of how the men in the family had stayed Amish and all of the women had left: Brother Joe sat at one end and Brother Simon at the other, representing the Amish part of the family, with Sarah, Susan, and myself and our spouses in between. I don't know if this says more about our family, or the community in general. Certainly the men in the community benefited more than the women from the requirement that women be subservient to their men—father, brothers, and husband. But we also had Mem's example to go by: she had stayed in a difficult relationship in which she was much more capable of taking the lead than Datt, yet this was unacceptable within the community. She had rebellious feelings about having to be subservient to someone who was unreasonable and less intelligent and capable than she was, yet she strove to conform to the Amish ways. Mem's true feelings about the treatment of women were not lost on us girls. But somehow I don't think even the most subservient of mothers would have made a difference for me. I would have needed to be endowed with a whole different personality to be able to conform to the Amish ways.

Joe sat with his head bent low, which was considered the humble Amish way, so that his chin was lost in his beard. His hair was cut in the Amish style, but it was unruly and stuck out on the sides, like many of the uncles and cousins on Mem's side of the family. Joe had a prominent overbite that had been one of his distinguishing features as a child. He was often teased for having "buck teeth."

There were many years in a row in which I didn't see Joe. I purposely avoided him—partly because I didn't trust him, and partly because I didn't know how to relate to him as an adult. When I saw him again three years ago, I was taken aback by how he had aged. He walked like Datt used to when he was an old man; he had a gray pallor, and his droopy eyelids obscured his dark eyes, but his nose was more like the pug nose from Mem's side of the family than the long, straight nose of Datt's side of the family. That Joe was sitting closest to Mem was symbolic of their relationship. Of all her children, Mem has always been the closest to Joe. She confided in him much the same way most women confide in their husbands, and much like most mothers confide in their daughters. I used to feel envious of their relationship.

Once, when Mem was talking with Joe in the room where she braided her rugs, I eavesdropped while laying in my bed in the room next door. Joe was about thirteen years old and I was ten. I heard the confiding tone in their voices, so I stayed quiet, thinking I would find out what they talked about when they were together. I heard Joe ask, "Why don't you go shopping with Datt?"

Mem sighed and settled into one of her stories that was meant for Joe's ears only. I felt like a sneak. I wondered if Joe knew I was there, on the other side of the curtained doorway that separated the two rooms.

"I used to go shopping before all the children came along. But now it's easier to let Datt do it. I didn't want to go anyway after Momme went through everything I had bought and told me all the things that I didn't need."

"Was this Momme on Datt's side?" Joe asked.

"Of course," Mem said. "My mem wouldn't do that."

"Why did you listen to her?" Joe asked. Then he suddenly walked over to the door between the rug room and mine, pulled the curtain back, and said, "Lomie, go downstairs!" He said it in an authoritative voice, as though he were my father. Because I was afraid to do otherwise, I got up from where I was lying on my bed, and as I walked down the back stairs, I heard Mem say, "I didn't know she was in there."

Joe said, "I thought she might be."

So Joe was Mem's confidant, and Mem was Joe's protector. Through many of his cruel episodes, she defended and supported him. He and Katherine are the only two children who got Mem's protection. It was understandable that Katherine got it, considering she was the most vulnerable of us all, but it often seemed as though Mem displaced the protection the rest of us needed by protecting Joe from taking responsibility for his own actions. Yet, there was one time when she failed miserably in protecting Joe, just when he needed it the most.

Joe was probably fourteen at the time. On this day, Mem had him chopping wood out by the driveway, to distract him from teasing and pestering the rest of us. When our midday meal was ready, Mem called to Joe to come in and eat. He didn't come. Mem looked out the window and saw that he was nowhere in sight, so she went out and called him, first towards the barn, then louder towards the woods. Still there was no answer. When Datt came in for *mittag*, Mem asked him if he'd seen Joe, and Datt said he'd seen him chopping wood out by the lane. Mem said, "That's what he was supposed to be doing."

We ate in silence, with Mem looking out the window every few seconds, as if she expected Joe to appear. After our meal, Datt hitched up the horse and buggy and drove down Durkee Road to look for Joe. The rest of us roamed the woods and called. No answer, and no sign of Joe. We came back, hoping Datt had found him. He hadn't.

At suppertime we still didn't have any idea where Joe was. By now Mem was crying. At bedtime we were out of ideas of where Joe had gone. Mem sent us to bed, but I couldn't sleep. I wondered if Joe had run away from home. He had often threatened to, when he and Datt had their disagreements. He had not yet fought back when Datt whipped him, but the tension between the two of them was getting to a point of snapping, like a rubber band stretched too thin. As I lay in my bed, wondering where Joe had gone, I heard Datt running out of the living room, through the kitchen, and down the stairs, with Mem right behind him. Datt said reprovingly, "Joe, where have you been? You had Mem worried."

Joe said, "It wasn't my fault." He was crying as he spilled out the story. He was chopping wood when two men in a pickup truck came along and asked him for directions to Forest Road. Joe had told them where it was, but they asked him to come with them to show them the way. Joe said, "But you'll have to drive me back if I come with you." They said they would, but then they kept driving right past Forest Road. Joe asked where they were going, but they wouldn't tell him and kept driving to a horse farm on Route 168.

"I kept telling them my family would be worrying about me, but they wouldn't listen," Joe said through his sobs. "They kept saying, 'You have to do this first,' then they would make me do something else after that."

"Who were these men?" Mem asked.

"Robley is the name of the man who owns the horse farm. I don't know the other man's name."

"Why didn't you come in and tell us you were leaving?"

"Because I thought I was only driving up to the corner and back!" Joe sobbed.

"What did these men want anyway?" Mem asked.

"They said they wanted to see if I would be a good worker at the horse farm. They did offer me a job."

"They did?" Mem asked.

"Why didn't they come ask us?" Datt asked.

"They said they wanted me to see the farm first, to see if I would want to work there."

"Would you want to work for them?" Mem asked.

"Not after what they did!"

"That's what I was thinking," Mem said.

Several weeks later, when a big white pickup truck drove in the lane and a man came to the door and asked Mem and Datt if Joe could work at Robley's horse farm, they said yes. If Mem put up any resistance to the decision, I don't remember it. Datt was thinking about the extra money Joe would be bringing in. He didn't seem to care that these same men had kidnapped Joe several weeks before. I rarely felt sorry for Joe, because he was so brutal, yet I couldn't believe Mem would let him go work for someone who was obviously dangerous. I knew there was something terribly wrong about allowing him to work for the men who had kidnapped him.

Joe worked on the Robley farm for part of the summer, and then someone in a white pickup truck showed up and dropped him off in the middle of the day. Joe was in tears, and he walked much like a child with a full diaper, or as if it hurt, like when he got a whipping from Datt. Joe never went back to work on the horse farm after that.

What happened to Joe while he was working for Robley is still left to my imagination. I believe whatever happened, it was probably repeated when he worked for John Roberts on his fruit farm. John Roberts was known to molest young Amish boys, who were prime targets for pedophiles, given they learned how to submit to authority figures.

I still wonder at my ability to forgive Datt for not protecting Joe in these instances, when it was obviously just as much his responsibility as Mem's. Perhaps it's because I had long before learned that I couldn't expect it from Datt—he seemed incapable of being a proper father. I expected more from Mem, however. Most of the time we relied on her to be the responsible parent, but such instances show how she seemed to have her motherly instincts all twisted up, like a clothesline that had to be untangled before it would be of any use. She wouldn't protect Joe from harm when he needed it the most, yet she'd protect him from his own actions, even when those actions hurt one of us.

I was often more afraid of Joe than I was of Datt, because Datt's violence was momentary; Joe's brutality was calculated and sometimes premeditated, and it was often couched in the mind games he liked to play with people, like the time when I was five years old and Joe was eight. He and a neighbor boy, Brian, had a bonfire going out in the yard between our houses. Joe called me, so I went over to see what he wanted. He smiled at me as he and Brian sat on a log beside the coals of their bonfire. Brian didn't look at me. He just kept his eyes on the coals. I saw he was looking at a little toy tractor, made of metal, resting in the smoldering gray ashes.

"Would you get that for me?" Joe asked, pointing at the toy tractor.

"It's hot," I said.

"No, it's not. I just put it in there," Joe said.

I folded my arms and said, "So, if it isn't hot, why don't you get it yourself?"

"Because if you do it, I will give you a roasted marshmallow," Joe said in a buttery voice, holding up a bag of marshmallows and a forked stick. I looked at the tractor, then at Joe, who was looking at me with those eyes that said, *Come on, you'll do it.* I looked at Brian again. I couldn't tell what he was thinking, but I didn't think he'd let me burn my fingers, so I reached for the tractor.

Just before my thumb and two fingers closed over the metal wheel, Brian said, "Don't touch it!"

He was too late. I had picked it up. The burning pain made me drop it instantly, and I looked to see if my fingers and thumb were on fire, they hurt so badly. I ran screaming for the house. By the time I got there, a blister had grown, big and white, on my thumb and two fingers.

I found out later that Joe had made a bet with Brian that he could convince me to pick up the hot tractor.

DAVID WHISPERED SEVERAL questions to me as we waited for the funeral service to start. He wanted to know who certain people were, and I told him. As I did so, the uncles and aunts on Datt's side of the family, who were seated directly across an aisle space from us, bowed ever lower, with their heads as close to their laps as they could get. After several questions, David sensed the tension and stopped asking.

Sister Sarah sat next to David, with her back straight. As a young woman, she had decided she was going to have good posture. Even during the three-hour church services, she would sit so straight that it looked like she had a yardstick stuck in her spine. Her hair hid the side of her face, but I knew she would have the pensive expression that new or stressful situations brought on. In most of her wedding pictures she had a pinched expression, as if she was holding back her feelings.

Sarah's straight back reminded me of the time she had openly defied Bishop Dan Wengerd. At the time, she thought she was about to make a public confession in church for smoking cigarettes. Cigarette smoking was forbidden for Amish women—the men were allowed to smoke a pipe and cigars, and cigarettes were discouraged but not forbidden for the men. In defiance of that double standard, Sarah and Susan had both taken up smoking. I didn't follow suit, because I felt they should pick their issues—smoking cigarettes to me was not a worthy cause.

I was at the service when Sarah was planning to make her confession. As was customary, she had left the room while the bishop discussed the "charges." I thought it was odd when Bishop Dan discussed other things besides the confession Sarah was prepared to make. He was concerned about her job as a landscaper because he thought it was not a good idea for her to work with men outside the community, "especially because they tend to take their shirts off, which doesn't make it a good place for an Amish woman to work."

He suggested that Sarah didn't need to make a public confession for smoking if she was willing to give up her job. The bishop sent the deacon around to collect all the expected yeses, and I said my yes because I didn't think I had any other choice.

When Sarah was brought into the living room, she was asked to sit before the bishop. He explained the terms to her. Sarah sat with a straight back, looking right at the bishop. Normally the repentant person was expected to look down in deference to the bishop. When he was done, he waited. Sarah straightened her back even more, if that was possible, and said, "I like my job, and I'd like to keep it."

Bishop Dan shuffled his feet and said, "Well . . . ahhh . . ." It was clear he had not been prepared for this response, so he had no idea how to proceed. "Okay, well, ah, I guess you need to take your seat, then," he said.

So Sarah had openly defied the bishop, even though, to my knowledge, she had never openly defied Datt. And then, ironically, what the bishop had warned would happen, did. Sarah became involved with one of the men she worked with, who got her pregnant, and then when he started physically abusing her, she broke off the relationship. Now she had a child to raise, and she had only Mem and Datt's house from which to do it—unless she left the Amish, which is what she finally did when her son was six years old.

Sarah's husband, John, sat next to Sarah. John also used to be Amish, though he had already left the Amish by the time they met. In fact, Sarah did what I vowed I would never do, even when I was still Amish—she married her second cousin. Our mother was a first cousin to John's mother. When I first found out that they were related, I laughed and said, "Sarah, you had the whole world open to you, and you came back and married your second cousin?" I thought she would laugh with me, but she didn't. I have learned not to talk about the issue at all anymore because of her sensitivity to it. She was the third of three of my siblings to marry a second cousin—Joe and Emma were second cousins, and so were Susan and Bill.

Susan sat next to John, with Bill next to her. Simon, the tallest in the family, sat next to Bill. He resembled Datt with his partially bald head and his large Roman nose, though he had Mem's blue eyes, and his beard had some red in it. Growing up, Simon seemed the most uncomplicated presence of all in the family. He expressed himself simply, and when conflict arose, he just disappeared. Years later I recognized that behavior, described in psychological terms as that of "a lost child." He did struggle, repeatedly, with Joe, but Mem always took Joe's side. When Simon was about eight years old and Joe was sixteen, it was their job to do chores each night. Almost every night, Simon would come in from the barn, crying and saying that Joe was being mean to him. Mem would tell him to go out and do what Joe said, and maybe he would stop hurting him. Simon would cry helplessly and plead with Mem, but she would insist he go back out to help with the chores. I wondered at the time what was going on in the barn. I thought about hiding there to find out, but I was too afraid of the consequences if Joe discovered me.

Because I no longer understood much of the Amish language, I had not been paying much attention to John Henry, my cousin, who was preaching the first sermon of the funeral. He had the physical characteristics of my mother's side of the family, with the bright red, almost orange, curly hair that stood out on the sides.

John Henry had all the mannerisms of a typical Amish preacher. When he first got up, he cleared his throat and grabbed the lapels of his jacket. He started talking slowly, clearing his throat and looking at the floor in front of him often. After several sentences, he looked up and around the room, and then he started pacing the floor. As he did so, his voice raised a bit, into a rhythm that was a sing-song.

Behind our bench sat our son Tim, my nieces and nephews, and my uncles, aunts, and cousins on Mem's side of the family.

There was a wide aisle in front of us, with the rest of the four hundred attendees facing us. Sam Kettie sat across from me. She had been married to Datt's brother Sam, and together they had fifteen children. Some years ago, Sam had died in a farming accident. Kettie had remarried, to a widower with seventeen children. Between the two of them, they had thirty-two children. At the time of their marriage, about half of their children were married and had left home.

Next to Kettie sat Datt's sister Sarah. She and Kettie both were bowing low, with their heads resting in their hands and their elbows resting on their knees. They clearly didn't want to look at us. Aunt Katie sat one row behind Datt's other siblings and their spouses. There was no mistaking those dark, piercing eyes, and the long, hawk nose. When John Henry talked about how it is never too late to come to God, her eyes raked across our bench at those of us dressed in "fancy" clothes. I looked back at her without fear or shame. When she saw me look at her, she quickly turned her head to look back at her lap. The all-powerful Aunt Katie from my childhood was powerless when I faced her as a self-assured adult.

After John Henry preached, Bishop Joe Byler got up to preach. He began with the traditional clearing of his throat, then he too raised his voice and paced the floor. He used tears to add to the fervency of his entreaties that we all be prepared to meet our Maker when our time comes. I preferred to think of Datt, who was the person this funeral service was for. I remembered the few times when Datt had obviously been right in his way of thinking, but had never gotten credit for it. As far as Mem and Joe were concerned, Datt could not be right, and he didn't have anything sensible to say.

One such instance occurred after Joe had been working with a carpenter's crew for several years. His boss, Eli Kauffman, wanted to move his family out of the house they were renting. Eli was a respected member of the community and an ordained minister in our church, as well as being the leader of a good, honest, hardworking carpenter's crew. He and his wife, Clara, wanted to buy a two-acre parcel of land on Forest Road from Mem and Datt, to build a house for their family. They were offering one thousand dollars an acre for the land.

Datt did not want to break up the forty-two-acre parcel he had bought before he and Mem were married. He could be stubborn about certain things, but what he was most stubborn about was parting with the land he was so attached to.

Mem and Joe thought Datt was being selfish. They wanted to sell it to Eli and Clara. They said such things as: "We owe it to them so they can stay in this community." "What have we done with that land lately?" "We need the money." "You just can't let go of your land." "Hanging on to your land is more important to you than having good neighbors."

Datt, for a change, had rational arguments. He said, "How do I know they aren't going to move to Michigan, like Joe Yoders and all the rest of them? Then they can sell it and we get high people for neighbors." And he simply said, "It's my land; I can do what I want with it."

I remember the day Mem and Joe wore Datt down. They were both coming at him with every possible argument. Datt sat on the rocking chair with his arms folded across his chest. He wasn't saying anything.

I had been observing the debate. I was mostly on Mem and Joe's side, partly because none of us ever stuck up for Datt. He was always wrong, after all. Deep down inside, a little voice was telling me that Datt had a point. But I also knew how much we needed the money, and I would have liked Amish neighbors because we had never had any that close before. It would be a short walk to their house through the woods.

Datt sat there, not saying anything. I thought he was being more stubborn than Mem and Joe put together. Then all of a sudden he scrambled to his feet, grabbed his hat, and made for the door, saying, "Sell the land then! You will anyway, no matter what I say!" He stomped out to the barn. I couldn't believe it. Datt had never given in like that before. Mem and Joe talked about how they thought Datt would change his mind again and not allow them to sell the land. I thought they were right.

We were all wrong. Datt didn't change his mind. I wondered why he had decided to sell the land, but I soon forgot about that when we had new neighbors.

Several short years after they bought the land from Datt, Eli and Clara moved their family to Michigan. Olin and Clara Yoder's son Andrew, and his new wife, Mary, bought it from Eli and Clara. Andrew and Mary sold the place to high people after living there for a year. Datt's predictions had all come true.

FROM THE TIME JOE first got a horse and buggy and started to drive around, he admired other boys' horses, especially the ones with their heads reined up high. Joe reined his horse's head higher than anyone I knew. Datt hated it, so sometimes Joe reined his horse in lower until he was out of sight, then got off the buggy to rein his horse in so high I wondered how the horse could run. Reining the horses' heads was designed to produce better posture. The young boys wanted sharp-looking horses, so they reined their horses in higher than their parents did. However, Joe reined his horse so high, it looked unnatural. It reminded me of someone running or walking while looking up at the sky.

I never knew where Joe got his first glimpse of the horse he wanted, but I do remember how much he wanted that horse. He immediately started campaigning for the money. Because Joe was not yet twenty one, he had to give the money he earned to Mem and Datt. As usual, Joe easily convinced Mem, but at least this time she didn't try convincing Datt and left that to Joe.

Joe's arguments were faulty but passionate. "This horse is so spirited, I'll never want another horse . . . this is the horse of my dreams . . . I do make most of the money that comes into this family," and on and on.

Datt's arguments were sound. "What's wrong with the horse you have? We had to sacrifice to buy you the horse you already have, why do we need to buy you another one? How do you know this horse trader is honest? How do you know the horse doesn't have *shtumba?*"

I didn't know what *shtumba* was, but Joe said, "Oh, no, I have checked the horse out thoroughly, and I know other Amish boys that have dealt with this trader." But, he couldn't give any reasons why the horse he already had wasn't good enough.

In the end, Joe bought the horse. When the horse was unloaded and walked around the yard, I knew why Joe had wanted that horse—he was the most beautiful horse I'd ever seen: sorrel, with two white feet on the right side and a big white star on his face. He held his neck up high, as Joe led him around, looking more pleased and smug than I'd ever seen him.

Two days later, Joe did not look pleased or smug. He sat on the couch, facing Datt sitting on his rocking chair in the living room, and admitted that the new horse did have *shtumba*, which was a cough from fungus in his lungs, caused by eating moldy hay or chewing on moldy wood. There was no cure for it.

Datt started in on his righteous lecture and eventually came around to saying, "You just don't know how good you've got it! If I had a father when I was your age, I would have respected him more than you do me!" And then came the predictable statement from Datt, "If my father hadn't died when I was thirteen . . ." His voice always rose and fell in the same places each time he said, "my father" and "I was."

"I can't help that!" Joe said loudly, bursting into tears. Then Joe began pointing out all Datt's faults. "It's also not my fault that your mother is the way she is. You always think we wouldn't be poor if your father hadn't died. If you weren't so lazy, maybe we wouldn't be so poor! If you had taught me the right way to do things, maybe I wouldn't have had to learn all on my own. You have never treated us children the way we deserve to be treated! And I hope if I ever get married, I don't treat my wife the way you've treated Mem." Joe went on and on, crying and spewing. I waited for Datt to pounce on Joe any minute; that would lead to one of their physical fights. Instead, Datt sat on the rocking chair with his arms folded across his chest and his mouth clamped shut. Then I realized it was because Joe was crying that Datt didn't fight. Datt never knew what to do when someone cried, and it somehow shut down his anger. Joe knew this and was using tears to say what he wanted. Until that moment, he had me convinced his tears were real, but now I realized just how good an actor Joe was.

Datt finally got up and walked outside. Joe stopped crying and told Mem he just couldn't help himself. Mem said with a sigh, "I know."

Joe kept his sorrel horse for less than a year before he moved on to his third one. By the time he got married and moved away from home, he had owned six different horses.

MY THOUGHTS CAME BACK to the funeral as people shuffled into a kneeling position. As we all knelt on the concrete floor, Bishop Joe read a long German prayer. Then everyone stood for a reading from the New Testament. After the reading, people quietly took their seats as the pallbearers moved Datt in his coffin outside the shed and opened it up. Rube's Dave directed the lines of people to file past Datt's coffin for the last viewing. After filing past the coffin, people gathered in the courtyard —the men on one side, the women on the other. He started with the people who had been sitting in the back; then Mem and Datt's relatives filed past the coffin. Finally there were only us children and our spouses and Mem remaining. We left our benches and encircled the coffin. Mem sat next to Datt's head and quietly looked at her husband's body for the last time. They had been married for fifty-one long, difficult years. I can count on one hand the number of times I witnessed a tender moment between the two of them. We all had something in common with her—a tumultuous relationship with the person who lay before us. Yet I could tell Mem felt sad. The tears I shed were for the sadness in the finality of the last good-bye, and the knowledge that for the rest of my life I would never see him or hear his voice again.

The four hundred people all dressed in black, encircling us in the court-yard, supported our grief as we quietly had our last moments with Datt. The courtyard was completely still: not a baby cried, not a bird sang. This moment that my sisters and I had dreaded, in which we thought our reactions would be watched and analyzed by our original community members, was transformed. All those years of judgment fell away, and in its place I felt supported by this community of people who had been there when I was growing up. The differences in the clothes we wore or what we believed didn't matter in that pregnant, quiet moment. Embracing one another in the Amish community was rarely done, but the effect of the support from this group steeped in community and tradition had a power of its own.

David Miller, who had been standing in the sidelines, came forward and closed the coffin. He screwed the lid shut, and then the pallbearers came forward and carried Datt's coffin to the waiting carriage and slid it in. Datt was about to have his last buggy ride. The week before, when he was on morphine and sleeping a great deal, he had related a dream he had in which he was planning to go to church, but there was no room on the buggy for him, so he couldn't go. It was one of the ways he had to let go of this life. He had already attended his final church service.

From those who were around him when he died, I heard descriptions of Datt's peaceful end. We had all hoped and prayed for this when we knew that

Datt was leaving us. The grace of a peaceful end to such a tumultuous life as Datt's was truly a miracle. Even though we had varying spiritual views, most people likely agreed that this was a sign of Divine Grace.

THE GRAVEYARD WAS SET UP on a hill above my Uncle Ervin's farm, with a row of pine trees marking the western border. When we walked up the long driveway to the graveyard, I realized the ceremony was almost over. The grave was nearly full as four men shoveled dirt into it. As they mounded the dirt, the Amish chant (much like a Gregorian chant) concluded, and Bishop Joe Byler read a German prayer. People bowed their heads in silence. After those gathered started moving about, Brother Joe pushed Mem in her wheelchair down to the little headstone at the edge of the cemetery, where Mem and Datt's stillborn baby was buried.

Rube's Dave walked towards David and me, and my thoughts came back to the present. He said, "You didn't make it on time."

"No, I underestimated how long it would take for everyone to get here." I introduced Rube's Dave to David and Tim. Dave's wife came over, and the five of us talked about Datt's funeral, about funerals in general, and about Dave's work as a funeral director in the community. He told me he and his wife had really enjoyed having me come visit them when I was a schoolteacher.

"I enjoyed those visits, too," I said.

Before Dave and Kate left the graveyard for a much-needed rest, they invited us to come and visit them when we come to Ohio again. I promised that we would.

As we left the graveyard, I looked back and saw the fresh mound of dirt that represented my father's final resting place, there on the outer edge of the cemetery above my uncle's farm. I sent my thoughts to the spirit who used to be Datt, and whispered, "Rest in peace."

SLEEP DID NOT COME to me for a long time that night. My mind drifted to my lifelong recurring dream, which most people would term a flying dream—but it isn't the high soaring flying of a bird, but more like the flight of a butterfly, light and floating just above the earth, landing lightly, and then taking off for another flight. Of all the feelings of euphoria I have ever experienced in my life, this dream is perhaps the most euphoric of all. I am always disappointed to awake and find I was merely dreaming.

I remembered a particularly vivid dream that started out as my euphoric dream and ended in a nightmare. In the first part of the dream, I was running with long, gliding steps just above the earth, then landing softly before I pushed off for another step or flight to my next landing place. I could make my steps last for as long as I wanted. My feet were my wings. I thought, "Oh, I have had this dream so many times and this time it's really happening! And this is even better than in my dreams!" I was sailing along, feeling the wind in my hair as it streamed out behind me. I had on a long, flowing gown, the color of a star in the night sky. I looked out ahead of me to the apple and peach trees on the hill. I could get there in two steps, or maybe three, when normally it would take two hundred.

I heard the breathing behind me before I knew Joe was chasing me. I was no longer running for the sheer joy of it. I knew as long as I kept running in this way he couldn't catch me. He knew that too. He also knew if I became afraid, I could no longer run that way. I felt his determination to catch me. Then I made the mistake of looking back. I landed heavily, my steps became ordinary, and he was nearly breathing in my ear. I awoke when he caught me—before the pain, but after the terror. As I listened to David's rhythmic breathing next to me, I was grateful that Joe no longer had power over me, and that I had the choice of returning to my present life of living in Vermont and attending Smith College, even though it seemed like that was a whole world away from me at that moment. Just like in the first part of the dream, I could avoid Joe's domination by floating lightly out of his reach, like the butterflies I used to try to catch in my childhood, when they would elude my hands.

When sleep finally came, it brought tumultuous dreams, from which I awoke and wept. I could not remember the content of the dreams, only a vague sense of being trapped. David woke up, and without a word, he held me. I clung to him, crying as I remembered the darkness of the dream and my childhood. David's arms around me were firm, supportive, and solid. Somehow our lips connected, and the kiss among my tears exploded into a bodily passion that shocked me—yet I had no choice but to go with it. As David's and my bodies moved together in a passionate rhythm, I wondered how I could experience such feelings in the face of death—on the same day that I had said my final good-bye to my father and had seen his body being laid in its final resting place.

After our passion was spent, David and I lay together with my body molded into the same shape as his. The rhythm of his heartbeat lulled me into a deep and restful sleep.

I've learned that people will forget what you said, people will forget what you did,
but people will never forget how you made them feel.
MAYA ANGELOU

Reckoning with Joe

n the morning, I asked David if we could visit my mother on the way out of Ohio. He said, "You realize we will be getting home really late, don't you?"

"Yes, but I just don't know when we will see her again."

"Okay, but it will be late by the time Tim and I get back to Vermont, after dropping you off."

"Would you want to stay in Northampton overnight?"

"No, I want to get back to work tomorrow morning. But we can stop by at your Mom's if you want. I will just count on this being a long day."

When we drove into the driveway of the farm where I grew up, David had the inspiration to knock on Joe and Emma's door and compliment them on their job of taking care of Datt on his deathbed, and for the arrangements of the funeral.

Joe quickly stamped out a cigarette when Emma opened the door and invited us in. I was happy he didn't do what he used to when we were young and I complained about the smell of his cigarette smoke. Then he would come and smoke into my face in response to my complaints.

Many people in the family and in my original community were of the opinion that Joe had changed over the years. Certainly there were outward signs of that—the farm was in much better shape than it had been fifteen years before. Back then, when David and I would go back to visit, we would find chicken feet and heads lying in the yard, and the animals showed signs of neglect. It all seemed to signify the depressed state of the owner of the farm. But over the years, all the farm buildings that were dilapidated and crumbling had been replaced with the new construction of a horse barn, buggy shed, and shop. Horses grazed in the fields behind the shop, creating a more picturesque view of the pasture than when we had two pigs, two horses, two cows, and one hundred chickens all competing for the same space.

Datt's funeral had been held in the shed the day before, but the people in the community had helped put back all the furniture in the house, and there were no traces left of the funeral.

David and I shook hands with Joe and Emma. We had had plenty of practice the previous few days. David said, "You both did a really good job with the funeral."

"Oh, we can't take credit for that; we didn't do any of it. The people in the community did it all," Joe said.

I said, "Well, even if you don't want to take credit for it, I thought it went really well."

"Yes, we have no regrets," Joe said. Then he changed the subject. "Are you going back today?"

"Yes, but I wanted to see Mem on our way back, and we thought we would stop in and say hello," I said.

"Well, I am glad you did," Joe said. "Come see us again sometime."

"Okay, we will."

David said on his way out the door, "I still say you did a good job." He and Tim had gone out the door, and I had my hand on the knob, when Joe asked, "Did you get to talk with many of the relatives yesterday?"

"Yes, I did. I found everyone really friendly. Even Uncle Gid was talking with David and me."

We discussed when the relatives would be returning to Wisconsin, New York State, and Kentucky respectively. I closed the door, and suddenly I found myself in a situation that I always told myself I would avoid—I was talking with Joe without David there as a support for me. But I took comfort in Emma's presence, and decided I could leave anytime if I felt the need to.

I became aware that Joe and Emma were both talking in English, and I said, "You two can talk in Amish if you'd like, but I might have to switch to English to respond."

"But I thought you didn't like that," Joe said.

I knew Joe was referring to a phone conversation from a few weeks earlier, when I had called to get information from him about Datt. This came from Sister Susan insisting that if I wanted information about Datt, then I needed to talk with Joe directly. There has been a major push from most of the members of my family for me to reconcile with Joe, and this was Susan's way of pressuring me. I then told her how Joe had refused to speak in English, forcing us to have a dual-language conversation, because I could understand what he was saying, but could not respond in kind. I said to Joe, "More of the Amish language has come back to me as I've heard it spoken these last few days. And yes, when I called here a few weeks ago and talked to you and you stayed with Amish, I was a bit annoyed, because I thought you were trying to make a statement by doing so." I realized that what I had told Susan had traveled back to Joe. I didn't like to have to defend myself to Joe for something I said to someone else. This was starting to bring back memories of Joe pitting one of us against the other when he'd play the game of "Who wants to be my little girl?" He would do this when one of us was at odds with him. The sisters would come running and crowd onto the little bench where he sat to play the game. He would rate them according to his mood: "Sarah is my little girl number one, Susie is number two, Lomie is number three, and Lizzie is not my little girl at all." Whoever was at odds with him at the time would not be his little girl. Later, he dropped the childish game, but he still would come and tell us his side of the story and hope to get us on his side. One such occasion was when he was being a "peeping Tom" while Sarah was planning to take a bath. She knew he was out there, and she pulled the curtain aside and yelled, "Joe!" He stepped down off the stool he was standing on, and tried to act innocent. Sarah yelled at him, and he came into the kitchen and said, "Sarah is accusing me of window peeping. Can you believe that? How would I even do that—the window is much too high!"

"Well did you?" I asked pointedly. He turned on his heel and walked out and said, "I am not going to waste my time with *you!*"

Whenever Joe had me singled out as his enemy in the days when we were still living at home, I would make a wish that we would all be upset with Joe at once, and he would have no one left on his side. I don't remember that ever happening. He was too good at getting us to "rat" on one another, and to win at least some of us over to his side of whatever argument was going on. As a matter of fact, Joe had a way of isolating the one person he was having an argument with, which only intensified the feelings of isolation and never being able to get even with him.

I changed the subject with Joe. "I should probably go over and visit with Mem, and then we need to get going home."

"I am glad we talked," Joe said. "I know you have had something against me all these years, and I didn't know how to change that."

"That is because a lot happened in our past, and you were pretty mean to me and the other siblings. I never heard an apology for any of it."

"I didn't know you needed an apology."

There was quiet for a moment, and then Joe said, "I am really sorry for all of it. I did a lot of things I regret."

"Do you remember that Saturday night when Mem gave you a haircut, when you got up and ordered me to clean up the hair? I swept it together, then I went to get the dustpan, and when I turned around, you had kicked the hair all over the kitchen again. You had that mean smirk on your face, and you said, 'Now clean it up again!' I was so mad at you, that I told you I was going to write a letter to Emma and warn her about you. I was drafting that letter in my head as I went to sleep that night, and then the next morning Mem told me I should do no such thing."

Emma laughed and said, "I would probably just have gotten really mad at you."

"I knew that you might, but I also told myself that you could never say that you weren't warned."

"You know, there are many boys who are really mean to their sisters, but when they grow up, the sisters learn to forgive and forget," Emma said.

"Emma, you don't need to defend me," Joe said.

Emma laughed nervously and became quiet.

"I also remember the times when I would run away from you and you would catch me, beat me up, and then when I was a crying heap on the ground, you would come up and kick me in the butt. That used to hurt so bad!"

"I am really sorry," Joe said. He had tears in his eyes, so I decided not to keep going. Joe's seemingly sincere apology registered with me, but I was not yet convinced that he had changed to such a degree that he would not still be deceptive and manipulate others. And it seemed he had the same ability to turn on the tears as Mem.

We were still unsure why Sister Katherine had not made it to Datt's funeral, and I had a hunch that Joe was behind that. But as in so many issues, I had no proof, so I could not accuse him. By the same token, these "hunches" prevented me from trusting Joe completely the way that Susan seemed to, and Sarah off and on.

"Thank you," I said. "That goes a long way."

"Good."

"I need to go and visit with Mem," I said. As I was leaving, Joe said, "I am glad we *talked*."

"Me too," I said in an even tone.

I walked to Mem's house, where she was sitting and talking with David and Tim. Her "English" friend, Rosie, was sitting by the kitchen table. She was a nurse who had helped care for Datt in his last few weeks. I gave Mem a hug and sat down in Datt's hickory rocker. I introduced myself to Rosie and invited her to come and join our visit, but she said she was giving us some space. I said, "It is really all right for you to sit with us." She finally did. Mem had been raving about how Rosie had been like a daughter to her for years. She did the same about Emma. Susan found it hard not to be envious of such sentiments, but I felt that Mem had a right to have as many surrogate daughters as she wanted—she had her surrogate daughters and I had my freedom.

Mem looked refreshed. She said she had slept well. She had been really exhausted the day before. Mem told the story about how Uncle Gid had brought a chair for her to sit in, but he had set it on the sidewalk so that it wouldn't sink into the wet and soft ground. He said to her, "I don't need to see moonshine in the daytime." We all laughed, and Mem's bosom bounced and her face got red. She always was amused by Gid's humor.

Joe sauntered in and began swatting flies that had gotten in the day before. He asked Tim if he was still in school, and Tim said he was going to college. Joe said, "Are you as smart as your mom? She is the smartest of us all."

"Oh, come on, Joe, there are plenty of smart people in this family. I am definitely not the smartest."

"Hey, if you can't take a compliment, I won't give you one."

"There is also such a thing as common sense. Intelligence without common sense is sometimes not very practical. In the Amish communities you find many smart people who have plenty of common sense. Then you have people who are highly educated without an ounce of common sense."

"You mean like a doctor who doesn't know how to change a flat tire, for example?"

"Something like that. Last week there was a nuclear physics professor at Smith who showed up to teach her class on the wrong day."

We visited a bit longer, and then David, Tim, and I excused ourselves and left for our journey home. I gave Mem another hug, a tradition I had started back when I had returned to the community after being away for four months. Judging by how heartily Mem hugs me back, I would say she likes this tradition.

DURING THE FIRST PART of our trip, David, Tim, and I talked about Datt's funeral and the visit to Mem's. Then Tim fell asleep in the back seat and we were quiet for a while. I thought about the apology Joe had made to me, and I honestly wished I could trust him. I remembered the summer I was eleven and he was fourteen, when he had molested me. That had severed any trust.

It all started one morning in late summer. Joe asked me if I wanted to help take the horses out to the pasture. We had a fenced-off place in the woods where the horses stayed cool during the day. Joe asked in such a nice way that I asked Mem for permission to go, and she said yes. Joe got up on Tops's back and I stood on a stump. He helped me up behind him.

I wore a black dress that someone else had made and given to us after her daughter had outgrown it. Mem used a lot more fabric and made the skirts more full, but this dress was what Mem called *eng*. My bare legs stuck out, and Joe kept looking back at them. It made me feel bare, so I tried pulling my dress down.

"My dress is *eng*," I said.

"*Eng*, what does that mean?" Joe asked in his too-smooth voice.

"It means the opposite of full. There's not enough material to cover my legs," I said.

"Well, what are you worried about? I am only your brother."

Of course he was my brother, but by the way he kept looking at my legs,

I still wanted to cover up. We rode in silence a while, and then he said, "You can hold onto me if you're worried about falling off."

I hadn't been worried, but when I looked down, I realized the ground was far away. Still, I felt safe on Tops's wide back. She was our trusty old workhorse—big, black, and gentle. Don plodded along behind us.

When we got to the pasture, he helped me get down, then swung his legs down and landed next to me. He took off Tops's bridle, walked her through the gate into the pasture, and let her and Don go off into the shade. After he closed the gate, he sat on the ground with his back up against the fence post and started rolling a cigarette. I didn't know that he smoked.

As he licked the paper, he said, "Lomie, have I ever told you I admire you?"

I looked down at my bare feet. I wondered what Joe wanted from me, because he would never give me compliments unless he wanted something in return. It made me uneasy, and I thought about turning around and walking back to the house.

"Do you know what admire means?" Joe asked.

"I think so." I did know what it meant, but I also knew Joe wanted to play teacher.

"When I say I admire you, it means I like you, and I like the way you do things."

I pinched my arms through my dress and didn't answer.

"Can I ask you a question, Lomie?"

"Yes."

"Do you know how babies are made?"

"Yes," I said hesitantly.

"Can I ask you another question?"

I didn't say anything.

"Can I do that to you?" Joe lit his cigarette under his droopy, sleepy-looking eyelids. He took a long puff to show me how well he smoked. I knew he wanted me to "admire" him, but I feared him instead.

"No. I don't want to have a baby," I said.

"Don't worry," he said. "I can pull it out before that happens."

Pull what out? I thought. Didn't men just touch women in their place? Or did they push it in? I didn't want to let on that I didn't know what he meant, so I said, "But I am only eleven years old; I'm too young."

Joe took another long puff on his cigarette and shifted his legs slightly, leaning more comfortably against his fence post and looking up at me.

"Did you know I've been doing it to Sarah?"

I knew that he knew I did, so wondered why he was even asking. I nodded.

"She's younger than you are."

"But I just don't feel right about it."

"You'll get used to it. We don't need to do it right now if you don't want. Mem said she wants us to go blackberry picking this afternoon. You and I could pick in a different place from the others. That way you can think about it first." He stood up and started walking in the direction of home.

All the way back to the house, Joe talked and acted as if we'd always been friends. It felt like a lie.

While everyone was getting ready to go berry picking, I offered to stay home and help Mem rip carpet rags, but she insisted that I go.

We all walked past the sugarhouse to the neighboring woods. We avoided the stinging nettles, stepped over a dead log lying over the path, and eventually came into the pasture where the cows grazed. We made sure there were no bulls among them.

Joe found a patch of berries and told everyone to pick there. He said, "Lomie and I will go that way and see what we can find." He pointed out towards a field away from the cows, where the grass was tall.

When we were in a place far enough from the others so we couldn't hear them, Joe said, "So, have you thought about what I said?"

"Yes."

"Well?"

"I don't want to. You are my brother. I don't think brothers and sisters are supposed to do that."

"But, that's all the more reason. You and I love each other. So it's an act of love."

I picked apart a leaf in my hand. It felt as though someone had reached in and tangled my insides. I could only think of a feeble protest. I said, "But, if that's true, then why was Mem so upset when she found out you and Sarah were doing it?"

"She doesn't understand that I need practice before I get married. You'd be doing me a favor, because I want to know how to do this for my wife someday."

"How do other people get practice?"

"I don't know about other people. I only know what I need."

I didn't say anything, but stared at the tall grass around my dress.

"You know, the others are going to wonder where we are pretty soon. If you don't want to, that's fine. I'll just get my practice from someone else."

I had so many mixed-up feelings, I didn't know what to do. I really didn't want Joe to go back to being mean to me. Maybe, if I agreed . . .

I asked, "So what do you want me to do?"

"Take off your underwear and lie down on the grass."

I did, with the *eng* black dress up around my waist. I felt like Katherine looked when she was three years old, having her diaper changed. Then Joe uncovered his penis. I could not believe my eyes. It was pale white, and so big it looked as though it belonged on a horse. All I could think of was how it would hurt if he tried to push it inside me.

From the woods, Lizzie called and said they couldn't find any more berries. I thought I was saved.

"Go towards that big oak; there should be some at the edge of the field!" Joe called.

In a moment, we heard their voices going in the other direction.

Joe lay on top of me. He tried to push his penis into me. It felt like a knife.

"Ow," I said.

"Am I hurting you?"

"Yes, you are. I don't think it will fit."

He stood up. There was blood on his penis. "Is that from you?" he asked.

"I don't know." No wonder it felt like he was using a knife.

He got out his red handkerchief and gave it to me. He let me clean the blood off myself, and then he cleaned himself. The others called again.

Joe said, "Maybe we need to give it up." He threw the handkerchief into the grass, pulled up his pants, and buttoned them. Then he turned and walked away.

On the way home, I walked as though my body wasn't mine. The sting and that awful, dry pain between my legs were not as bad as the feeling that Joe had hurt a place deep inside I didn't know was there.

Somehow I walked home. I went right to my room, curled into a tight ball on my bed, and cried.

Sometime later, Mem came up to my room. "Lomie, what's the matter?" When I rolled over, I could see flour on her apron from the pies she was making with the berries.

"Are you sick?"

I shook my head, then nodded.

"What's wrong?"

I couldn't lie. "Joe—bothered me. In the blackberry patch."

Mem got quiet for a moment; then she asked, "Well, why did you let him?"

Mem's words struck me like whip. I retreated to the outhouse and sat there crying into my hands. I hadn't expected Mem to make the hurt feel better. No one could do that. But I hadn't expected her to make it go deeper, either.

Mem called my name from the kitchen window. I managed to catch my breath, and decided to pee before I went out. The second I started, I screamed. It felt like someone had stabbed me with a hot needle. I stopped and didn't want to pee, ever again.

"What's wrong, Lomie?" Mem asked. She had come out when she heard me scream. She opened the door and looked at me. She asked, "What's the matter?"

"It hurts to pee!" I gasped.

Mem looked worried. She said, "But you can't hold it back, either. That would make you sick."

I waited until hours later, when I could wait no longer. It was so painful, I felt like I would die.

The next day, Mem asked me in an anxious whisper, "Does it still hurt when you pee?" I said no, even though it did. I cringed each time, until it finally stopped hurting, several days later.

THE MEMORY OF THIS event makes me as angry with Mem as I am with Joe. Perhaps she did reprimand him when I was not around, but she never retracted her question that essentially blamed me. And what made it worse was that Joe had made a show of giving me a choice. I wished I had said no, because the consequences of that could have been no worse than what they turned out to be—unless he had forced himself on me. But now I realized the coercion was as psychologically damaging, if not more so, than the physical force would have been. In remembering this, I still wish I had not "let him." As it is, I will forever blame myself. The focus is not on the act of Joe putting me in that position, but rather my "consent" that I gave out of fear. Joe was always very adept at deflecting the blame for his wrongful activities away from himself. When he shot Shep, our family dog, he claimed it was because Datt told him to do it. It is true that in those days it was acceptable to get rid of the dog when the neighbors complained that our dog had wandered the neighborhood and impregnated their dog. Of course, another acceptable solution was to train our dog not to wander the neighborhood, even if we had to keep him chained.

Joe told the story afterwards of how he took Shep into the woods, and when he pointed the rifle at Shep, the dog tilted his head and wagged his tail, as if he was asking why this was happening. Joe then ended the story by saying, "It was everything I could do to pull that trigger." This was designed to get us to feel sorry for Joe, not the dog. It must have been effective for everyone else in the family, because no one else blames Joe for having shot Shep. However, the two details I will never forget are that Joe had a brand new rifle at the time, and that he never even bothered to bury Shep. His blond fur and bones lay in the thicket in the woods for a long time. I never liked walking by there. It was too creepy.

Joe seemed to want to dominate animals the way he dominated people. Not long after he shot Shep, he brought home Spike. Joe first encountered Spike when he was walking out across a field, near one of the houses where he was working with the carpenter's crew, when this German shepherd dog came up and growled at him. Joe kept on going, as if he wasn't afraid, and Spike came up and planted himself in front of Joe's legs and wouldn't let him move ahead.

Perhaps it was the challenge of gaining control over an intelligent and powerful animal that intrigued Joe. I don't know what deal he made with Spike's owner, but he brought Spike home as his own dog several weeks later. Spike had a vicious bark and lunged on his chain whenever visitors arrived. He was usually chained to the woodshed door. The number of visits from our friends dwindled.

Spike was very protective and loyal to all of us in the family. One day he actually protected me from Joe. The incident leading up to it actually had to do with Mem and Datt, but as usual, Joe got involved.

It all started one day during *mittag* when I was alone with Mem and Datt, the first fall after I graduated from eighth grade and could no longer go to school. Mem had made a stew the night before that tasted to me like pig slop, and I told her so. She hadn't said anything, but I could tell by her slumped shoulders that I had hurt her feelings. She was warming it up for our lunch. I complained and asked if I could make myself something else. She grudgingly said yes. I made *rivel* soup for myself, which is a milk-based soup with drops of a mixture of eggs and flour. The soup thickens a bit and the lumps of egg and flour cook to taste like noodles. *Rivel* soup rarely tasted so good to me as I tested it for the right amount of salt and pepper. I had my own nice bowlful, just the right consistency. I put it at my place at the table. I sat with Mem and Datt as we did our *Händt nunna.* The soup smelled warm and good.

Datt raised his hands off his lap, grabbed his glass of water, and took a drink. Then he asked, "What is that?" as he pointed to Mem's stew.

"Leftovers from last night," Mem answered.

"What's that?" Datt asked, as he pointed to my bowl.

"*Rivel* soup," Mem said.

"I'd rather have *that,*" Datt said, pointing to my bowl again.

Mem reached over and took my bowl of soup and put it in front of Datt. I sat there and stared at the empty place where my bowl had been and felt my anger build up into a rage. I imagined grabbing that bowl of soup and pouring it over Datt's bald head, since he wanted it so badly. Maybe I would save half to pour on Mem's head and watch it drip down over her head covering. Instead, I got up from my place at the table to make more soup. I slammed the cupboard doors. Each bang released only a little of my anger, which I felt as a heavy pressure in my chest. Mem said, "Lomie, you better stop that if you know what is good for you!" in her solid voice. I left the house because I didn't trust myself, or Mem and Datt, if I threw a chair through the window, which is what I felt like doing.

I didn't have a direction, but I walked the path through the woods that went out to Forest Road. I clenched my fists and wanted to scream, *How dare they? One of them is as bad as the other. I'd rather have that, indeed!* I gritted my teeth together, thinking, *Mem pretends she is on our side when we talk about how unfair it is that men are the boss of women and girls. Now I know the truth!*

I imagined myself going out on Forest Road and hitchhiking far away, to anywhere. I kept walking in that direction. I came to the edge of the field, and there I lost my courage. I sat down in the high grass under a maple tree and pulled a weed and chewed on it. I had forgotten until then how hungry I was. Still, I vowed I was going to stay away from home long enough to make them think I had run away, since I didn't actually have the guts to do it. I heard a car on the gravel road, then the smooth sound of the tires when it hit the paved road at the township line. The township line was on the bend in the road, just before the car came into my sight. The car passed by the line of trees along the road. The colorful branches looked as though they were moving as I watched the car pass. While it was visible, I didn't feel alone. It passed out of sight, and I listened to the whir of the tires on the pavement until I could no longer hear it. Then I was alone again. A bee buzzed around me and I held still. It buzzed off into the middle of the field. I lay down and looked up into the red, gold, and green branches of the maple. I looked at the pattern of the maple leaves, and then I dozed off.

At dusk I slowly awoke to the sound of Joe calling me from far away. There was a soft rain falling. I didn't answer. I hoped if I stayed still, he wouldn't find me. He came closer, calling out my name. I lay still. Spike was with him, and he came over to me and sniffed my face and wagged his tail. I knew Joe would find me now. I sat up.

"Why didn't you answer me?" Joe asked.

"I was sleeping," I said.

"Then what woke you up?"

"Spike put his wet nose in my face."

"You mean you didn't hear me call you?"

"No," I lied. I hoped Joe wouldn't press me on it. He had a way of proving my lies, then punishing me. This one he couldn't prove unless he got me to admit it. I was determined not to. I'd use his example and look him in the eyes and lie with a straight face if I had to.

Joe said Mem and Datt were worried about me and we needed to go home. I knew I had no choice except to walk home with him. As we walked past the trash pile with Spike walking alongside us, Joe said, "You should be thanking me for finding you."

I said something defiant without thinking, and even as I said it the fear crept up my scalp and prickled at the top of my head. I said, "Yeah, what if I am not thankful, then what?"

Joe stepped in front of me and slapped me across the face. Spike growled. Joe looked at Spike and said, "Spike, it's okay." Spike's hair stood up on the back of his neck and he growled at Joe again.

Joe started walking really fast, away from Spike and me. I petted Spike's back and said, "Good boy, Spike." I purposely lagged behind Joe. By the time I got home, he had already told Mem and Datt he had found me. I went straight to bed without eating supper.

THE ONE TIME JOE could not shove the blame on anyone else was when his rabbits died. Several years ago, I wrote down my memories of this incident and sent it to Mem. Her response was telling. She wrote back that she had cried for three days. Joe finally got the story out of her about why she was so sad. She later said to me, "He helped me realize that this happened a long time ago, and that he was a mere school boy, different from who he is now. I burned your letter, because I didn't want to think about it anymore."

The summer I was ten and Joe was thirteen, my sisters and I noticed that when we came near the rabbit pen where Joe's two young bunnies lived, they would beg us for food. One afternoon, Sarah and I were gathering chamomile near the chicken coop, for food to play "house" in the corncrib. The chickens made their afternoon noises, "bawk, bawk, baawk . . ." The pigs grunted in their pen behind the chicken coop, and the horses stomped in their stalls every so often to keep the flies off their shoulders, where their tails couldn't reach. Beside the chicken coop was a rabbit pen made of the same wire mesh as the walls of the corncrib. Both a white bunny with pink ears, and a coal black one lived in the pen. They begged us for food by standing on their hind legs at the cage door, twitching their noses. They crawled over one another in their eagerness to eat the pig's ear leaves, clover, and lettuce we gave them. They ate quickly and begged for more. We could not figure out why the rabbits were so hungry. We thought Joe was feeding them, because they always had water in their bowl, and feeding and watering went together. We thought they might be sick, because they looked so thin under fur that had lost its luster.

One day, I asked Joe why his rabbits were so hungry.

He demanded, "Have you been feeding *my* rabbits?"

I thought about lying, because I could imagine the slap across my face if

I told the truth. I also thought about trying to run away from him, but I knew he liked that because he could show me how much stronger and faster he was.

"Yes," I said.

"You *stop* feeding those rabbits! Those are *my* rabbits!" Joe said, with such vehemence I knew I wouldn't be feeding them again.

I didn't go near the rabbit pen again.

One day, as I sat at the round oak table in the kitchen, eating Mem's warm buttermilk cookies, I heard that Joe's rabbits had died. When I heard how they died, I stopped chewing and felt like I was going to throw up. Joe had been doing an experiment to see how long it would take for rabbits to starve to death.

I left the cookie on the table and walked numbly out of the house and into the woods, past the compost pile by the rotted stump, then past the leaf pile, without thinking about where I was going. When the shock wore off, tears came—quietly at first, and then they built up. I fell to my knees in a thicket, and my sobs nearly choked me. I hugged myself and rocked back and forth. "Why didn't I feed them?" I asked out loud. Then my crying came from down deep, pushing up through my throat in long, keening wails. I was more afraid of Joe than ever. If he could kill rabbits, could he also kill me? Maybe one of these times he would beat me so hard, I would die.

As I remembered the fear of that afternoon, I must have made an audible sound, because David asked me, "What are you thinking about?"

"I was remembering the things Joe has done in the past."

"Like what?"

"Like the time he starved his rabbits and the time he molested me."

"What brings that to mind?"

"Because after you left, Joe apologized for the things he has done in the past."

David said, "Wow, that's a big thing. Has he ever done that before?"

"No."

"Do you think he was sincere?"

"If I go by his tears and the emotion with which he said it, yes. He was most likely sincere, at least in the moment. But then again, I remember times in the past when he used his tears as a way to get what he wanted. He clearly wants me to forgive and pardon him for the things he has done in the past. I think what he really wants is for me to trust him, too."

"And do you?"

"I certainly do not pardon or trust him. And it depends on one's definition of forgiveness, as to whether I forgive him. The Amish definition is to 'forgive and forget.' By that, they mean that you wipe the slate clean, and you give the person the same chance to do better as if they had done no wrong in the first place. In other words, you are required to trust that person. To me, this seems as if you are making yourself vulnerable for more hurt. I like the definition of forgiveness that my counselor taught me—that you basically forgo or give up the right to hurt back the person who hurt you. By this definition, I have forgiven Joe. I wish him no ill, but it does not mean I trust him. In order for me to fully forgive or trust someone after I have been wronged, I have to understand how it came about that the person did what he did by putting myself in his shoes. I now understand how it was that Datt became violent, for example. He literally could not do anything differently than he did, with his mental illness and his level of intelligence. But for some reason I have never been able to put myself in Joe's shoes or understand why or how he could do all the things he did."

"What do you consider the worst thing he has done?"

"To me or to someone else?"

"Let's start with you."

"In terms of cruel, it was the beatings he used to give me. Then, when I was lying on the ground in a painful, crumpled heap, he would kick my butt so hard, I felt it all the way up my spine, into my head. And then there was the incest. That is never an easy thing to recover from. And of course the secretive, closed Amish system makes it even harder."

David asked, "And what is the worst thing you know of that he did to someone else?"

"To animals, it was starving the rabbits. To a person, I would have to say molesting Katherine. He molested all of us, but Katherine was the most vulnerable. And she is the only one who got pregnant. And I still think it was he who got her pregnant. Katherine claimed several years later that is who did it, even though she told us at the time it was Joe Basco, the Yankee guy who used to come visit our family on a regular basis. Joe told her to name him when she was asked."

"Didn't someone tell you that Joe admitted it to the bishop once?" David asked.

"Yes, but I have never been able to confirm that. If that is true, I wonder what the bishop had over Joe? He would not reveal what I think are his deepest, darkest secrets unless there was something worse hanging over his head."

"Yes, but with the Amish definition of forgiveness, it doesn't matter how bad the offense is, he would still get the same blank slate as someone who is being forgiven for getting drunk or something, right?"

"Yes, and therein lies the problem of accountability. If Joe is still not being held accountable for his actions, can he be trusted to do the right thing, when the crooked or dishonest thing will suit him better? I don't know that he has changed to that degree."

David didn't respond, and I was quiet for a moment. Then I continued. "And that is the other thing about forgiveness—I can forgive Joe for the wrongs he did me, but I am in no position to do that on Katherine's behalf, especially since he has never even come clean with an acknowledgment that he did take advantage of Katherine when she was a mere sixteen-year-old. With her mentality, it was more like having sex with his ten-year-old sister. I don't actually know how I could forgive him for that—it seems to me it would require acknowledgment, atonement, and restitution—and not just for Katherine, but for her son, too. Paul Henry is no more able to take care of himself than Katherine is. It sounds like the Amish couple that adopted him did not know how to handle him. The Mennonites are certainly charitable in caring for him, but I wonder what would happen to him if that changed?"

"Remember the look on Joe's face when the Mennonites showed up with Paul Henry last summer?"

"I sure do! I have never seen Joe so embarrassed and humbled in my life! I bet Joe would have said no to the leader of the group, when he asked if the young people could sing for them, had he known that Paul Henry was among them."

"I bet so too."

"As it was, Joe pushed that decision off on Mem. He thought Mem would resist making the decision, but she said, 'If it's up to me, then I want them to sing.' When Paul Henry walked up, the last in the group of young people, and Mom said, 'Here is my grandson,' it took me a moment before I even understood who he was. I think it was Joe's expression that made me realize this was Katherine's (and probably his) son. I have never seen Joe's eyes try to bore a hole in the ground, so he could crawl in and hide, like they did that afternoon."

"Was Paul Henry at your dad's funeral?"

"No, but he came to the wake. I could tell Joe was very uneasy when he was in the living room. He found a reason to leave."

"But wasn't there the time that Katherine actually did tell on Joe for molesting her?"

"Yes, that was after she'd been pregnant, which makes what Joe did even worse. She was going down to his and Emma's place to help out with the farm chores, and he was taking advantage of her. He was already the father of three or four children at the time. And the only reason she told on him is because he stole seventy dollars from her purse, which she had spent untold hours to earn. So, from this experience, we know that he did molest her, whether or not he fathered Paul Henry."

"The problems in your family are so complex," David said.

"Yes, aren't you so glad you married me? Look at what you would have missed if you hadn't."

"Oh, yes, I am so lucky." David looked at me sideways, with a grin on his face. I laughed with him. Then he said, "You are waiting for me to say it is all worth it, aren't you?"

"Not if you don't mean it," I laughed.

"Hey, I pursued you when you went back to the Amish, didn't I?"

"Yes, when you were in your twenties; but that doesn't say whether you are glad or sorry for doing it now."

"Hey, I knew what I was doing."

"I think that is the closest you are going to come to saying you are not sorry. I should probably stop there."

"Yeah, don't push your luck." David opened his window as he approached the tollbooth near Buffalo. I yawned. "I am so sleepy. Do you mind if I take a nap?"

As I closed my eyes, I thought about how the distance, represented by the miles of highway, is the only physical aspect that separates me from the community where I grew up. I was glad for the trip to make the psychological shift between the horse-and-buggy world I had left twenty-four years ago, and my present world of Smith College. My mind drifted back to the days when Joe was a teenager and had established complete dominance over my sisters and me.

In the Shadows of the Buggies

One Monday morning, when Joe was about eighteen years old, he didn't get up when his ride came to take him to work, so the carpenter's crew left without him. Joe had been out partying the night before. I dreaded the day, because I knew he would be in a foul mood. I decided to lay low and not get in his way. He was sleeping on the couch when Mem let him know *mittag* was ready. He groaned and did not get up. So the rest of us ate, then we bickered about who had to do the dishes and who had to sweep the basement floor. There were few tasks I hated more than dishes, but sweeping the basement floor was one of them. In the end, I had to sweep the floor. The dirt stuck to the rough cement, so it was hard to sweep. Mem often told the story of how she was nearly nine months pregnant with Joe when she laid the cement. She stood on a board and used a trowel to smooth it out. I wondered why she had used cement with such big stones in it, rather than fine sand. Most likely it had been cheaper, and it was all she could afford.

I had started by the canning shelves, and had made my way over near the steps when I heard footsteps going from the living room into the kitchen upstairs. They stopped right above me, then Joe said, "What's for *mittag?*" The desire to lay low and stay out of his way melted as I felt my anger rise. The thought of Mem telling me to make *mittag* for Joe was too much. Before I could check my anger, words came tumbling out of my mouth: "Maybe if you weren't such a lazy sleepyhead you would know that!"

Joe's heavy, deliberate footsteps came tromping towards the kitchen door. I could hear his brutality in every footfall as he stomped down the stairs. Not fast, but slow, like he wanted me to feel the anticipation of getting hit as long as he could. I thought about running out the basement door, but he was faster than I was. Running for the outhouse had stopped working ages ago. I had only one option left. I called for Mem.

She didn't respond.

Joe marched up to me, stood there, raised his hand, and hit me across the face. My glasses fell to the floor. Then, with his other hand, he hit me on the other side of the face, just as hard. I screamed.

Joe turned and started walking up the stairs.

I picked up my glasses and found they were broken. I hated Joe more than ever. "You broke my glasses!" I bellowed. "Now you can pay for them!"

Joe stopped on the stairs, turned around, came back down, and slapped my face so hard I felt a jolt in my neck and heard it crack. I wanted so much to slap him back, slam the broomstick across his head, punch him, kick him, do whatever I could to hurt him. But he was the Almighty Joe. I screamed out my rage. I knew it could be a long time before I would have those glasses fixed or get new ones. It had taken Mem and Datt six years to get me glasses after the teachers in public school advised that I should have my eyes checked. Now I would have to do without glasses again, because I had let Joe get me upset enough that I could not stay quiet, when I knew that the result of my outburst would be a beating. And Mem's response, if I complained, would be, "Well, Lomie, you always *do* need to learn the hard way!" She, of course, meant that I should learn how to control my anger and not say anything to Joe that would trigger his brutality. But, I wondered, how could I rein in my rebellion when there was no justice in my life—when I did not have even one person I could count on to stand by me when I needed it the most?

IF I THOUGHT JOE HAD dominated me when he first began his *rum springa* years, I would find him increasing that a notch when I myself joined the young people. *Rum springa* (running around) in my home community was not a time for young people to go out and try new things and then decide whether they would stay in the community, but rather it was a time of courting within the community, in which some parents looked the other way when their young people were playing music, dancing, visiting bars, and drinking. And like their parents before them, they looked the other way when their daughters brought young men home and went to bed with them. Bed courtship has been used since before the Amish ancestors emigrated from Europe. In those days, it was called "bundling," with a board placed between the man and the woman. It is believed that this method of courting began during the time our ancestors were being persecuted. This allowed young people to hide from the authorities in upstairs bedrooms, which were often cold, so it allowed both people to stay warm under the bedcovers while "visiting." Many generations ago, the board disappeared, leaving the bed courtship rituals. Even the Amish are embarrassed to talk about this practice, because it is hard to explain to outsiders that they are not encouraging their young people to have sex, even though they allow them to go to bed together. The obvious question is, of course, how does one know whether they do or not? It seems every young woman has to decide for herself where her boundaries are. This is tricky business—there is little room between gaining a reputation for being "easy" and gaining the reputation for being "frigid." Most young women wait until they are married to become pregnant, but by no means all.

When a young woman does get pregnant before she is married, the couple is expected to marry. But before they can do that, they need to be members of the church. This means that if they haven't already "joined church," they now need to make haste to do so. Most of the time, it takes a whole summer for young people to receive instructions for baptism, partly because each district holds services every two weeks. The baptismal service is then held once a year, in the fall. Young people preparing for their "shotgun" wedding now have to receive instruction from their own district as well as a neighboring one (thus attending church every Sunday during their instruction period), and then a special baptismal service is held to baptize the young person or persons, so that the woman getting married can do so before her pregnancy becomes obvious to others.

Outsiders often ask: why tempt the young people in this way? Even some Amish people feel this way, and their beliefs generate start-up communities; it is impossible to change the ways in an established community in which this courtship ritual has been practiced for generations. One such community is in Mio, Michigan. Many of these church members moved out of our church district when that community was established, back in the 1970s.

All during the *rum springa* years, the parents keep a close eye on their young people for signs that they are *unzufriede* (discontent) with the Amish ways. So, dating someone outside the Amish, taking a course at a college, taking trips alone far away from home, or deciding to go out for dinner on dates instead of practicing bed courtship would be more threatening to most parents than getting drunk on a regular basis, driving buggies while drunk, or becoming pregnant, even though pregnancy before marriage is a big embarrassment.

The venue for dating is at the gatherings for the young people. There are two basic kinds—"parties" on Saturday nights, and "singings" on Sunday nights. The "singings" are acceptable to all parents, while some parents will not allow their young people to attend the parties. The only difference between the two, besides being held on different nights of the week, is that at the singings, the young people sit in rows in the kitchen of the houses where the singings are held (usually this family has held church in their home that day) and sing songs before the music, dancing, and drinking begin out in the barn. At the parties, the singing part is skipped. It is around the dancing in the barn that young Amish women are taken aside and asked for dates—not directly from the young man, but rather from whomever he chooses to send as his emissary.

So when I started my *rum springa*, I became dependent on Joe to take me places, because he had a horse and buggy and I didn't. Most young men are expected to take their sisters along to the singings, but Joe had managed to escape the "embarrassment" of taking Lizzie when she reached the normal age for dating, except for a very few times when Mem had insisted. The few times he did take her, he stranded her at the singings by having a date. Lizzie had made a friend during these few outings, and so she would go and spend the night at Amanda's house when Joe abandoned her. To my knowledge, Lizzie never had a date within the Amish.

Joe was going steady with Emma by the time I joined the young folks, so I often got a ride to her house with him on Sunday afternoons as I became friends with Emma's two sisters, Ada and Ella. We would find a way to the singing from their house together. They lived in a more central place in the community, which meant that we could often walk to the singings or catch a ride with the young men in their neighborhood. I didn't plan on joining the young people when I did. I backed into it, so that I could hardly point to the time I began my *rum springa*. One Saturday night, when I was seventeen, one of my second cousins invited me for an overnight stay. They lived down on

Donley Road, close to my grandparents. Whenever we visited them (Momme and Dodde), we would visit the Andy Millers'. We had known this family ever since we were little children. They once lived on Route 608, several miles from us, and our families would walk crosslots through the woods to visit one another. Andy Em and Mem are first cousins, so my friend Mary and her siblings are fifteen of several hundred of my second cousins on Mem's side of the family.

Mem said I could go to Mary's house for overnight. I had a problem. I didn't have an appropriate nightdress. Mem hadn't let me make one yet. Nightdresses were made in the same pattern as our day dresses, except they had buttons down the front instead of pins. Mem insisted I take one of her nightgowns, which I could have fit into twice. When I shamefully showed it to Mary, she found one of her sisters' nightdresses and let me borrow that.

Mary and her sisters had invited several of their other friends, including Lizzie and Lucy, who were sisters.

I was invited to more gatherings after that first night. Mary and her friends taught me how to do the square dance that was customary at the singings. It was basically made up of walking up and back, arm-in-arm with one's partner, then splitting off, going around the person next to one's left, and swinging with one's partner. It was a boring dance, but given it was the only dance the Amish used, I got into the swing of it. Girls always started out the dance at the singings, and sometimes boys would cut in to dance with the girl of their choice.

Lucy was one of my favorite partners, because she and I did the swinging well together. There were boys that came to the group get-togethers too, but I told myself they were there because of Lizzie, Lucy, and Mary. A homely boy named Freeman often cut me out in dancing, so he could dance with Lucy. I'd look at the two of them together and wonder what she saw that she liked in him, because she had all the beauty he lacked. Her skin looked clear in the light of the lantern, and her blue eyes became the color of the clear sky when he danced with her.

Soon after I started hanging out with this group of young people, I started going to the singings. That night, Mary's sister Ada took me aside and asked me, "Is it all right for Gid tonight?" I waited, thinking she would finish her question. She was looking at me in the darkness of the yard, next to shrubs. I said, "What?"

"Gid is asking you for a date," Ada whispered. My stomach did a flip inside me as I realized what she was saying. Then a nervous fluttering feeling started from my overturned stomach. Gid was one of the boys who came to the group get-togethers. I was surprised that anyone would ask me for a date, because I saw myself as fat and ugly. *I am one of Sim's girls and I might not have very many chances for dates*, I told myself as I said, "Yes." Then as soon as Ada left, I wished I had had more time to think about it. I was not the least bit attracted to Gid. In fact, I found him downright homely. I thought about finding Ada and telling her I didn't want to have the date with Gid after all. Then I realized how awkward that would be at the get-togethers after that, and left it alone.

In the Amish tradition, Gid did not need to ask me for a date directly. By having someone else ask for him, he could avoid a potential rejection. I had known this, but when Ada had asked me in that way, she still had to explain to me what she was doing. It had never dawned on me before, but this system of sending an emissary to ask for him was cowardly. But then again, I told myself, it could have also protected me from saying no to him directly. Somehow it seemed more of a protection for him than me, though.

At ten-thirty Ada told me Gid was ready to go. She walked me to his buggy and disappeared into the darkness. I climbed onto the buggy, Gid clicked to his horse, and we drove into the night. The nervous fluttering feeling in my stomach got worse as Gid and I made small talk. I sat tensely on the seat of his buggy as we drove past the dark homes on Clay Street. Most of them were Amish, but there were a few English homes, too. I didn't know what to expect once we got to our house. I knew the Amish used bed courtship, but I didn't know the details. Most girls probably learned this from their older sisters, but because Lizzie had never had a date, she couldn't fill in these details for me. Does he leave his clothes on? I wondered. Am I supposed to leave the light on or blow it out? I wondered how I was supposed to know these things, and whether other mothers told their daughters more about this. Or did they learn it from other girls, or the dates themselves? So far, Gid had not said a word about it.

When we got to our house, I told Gid which way to go to get to the right room, and told him I would have the light on. I ran upstairs and got into my pink nightdress that I had made the week after the embarrassing night at Mary's house. I sat on the side of the bed, waiting for Gid to come in. I wondered if Mem or Datt heard him in the barn, or if they were too sound asleep. I knew I would get teased about having a date the next day if anyone in the family found out. They expected I would eventually have a date, but they didn't know when or with whom. And Mem and Datt were expected, like other parents in the community, to ignore any sounds they might hear in the night, including the sound of a stranger's footsteps on the stairs on his way to their daughter's bedroom.

Gid came slowly up the stairs, through Joe and Simon's room, and opened my door. He took off his hat, then his shirt, leaving his white T-shirt on. Then he took off his shoes, leaving his pants and socks on. He pulled the bed covers back and got in on the other side of the bed. I got in on my side and lay on my back, stiff and tense. I wondered whether I was supposed to blow out the lamp, but since Gid didn't say anything, I didn't. We lay there. I was thinking to myself, if he tries to *shmunzle* (hug and kiss), then I will have to let him. I knew young people would sometimes *shmunzle* when they were alone. I had seen several couples at the singing that night, *shmunzling* in the shadows of the buggies. But I had no desire to be touched in any way by Gid.

At some point, Gid took his arm out from under the covers and laid his hand over the covers, on top of my stomach. I tensed even more. He left his hand there for a while, and then he took it away. He left for home around one o'clock in the morning. I thought that was an unusual time for him to leave. I thought most of the time young men leave for home around four o'clock in the morning. I didn't understand why until the following weekend, at my second singing.

I was sitting on Gid's buggy with Lizzie. She asked me how my *shnitz* went (*Shnitz* is what the Amish call a first date.)

I said, "Okay."

Lizzie giggled behind her hand. "I laughed when I heard about it," she said.

"Why? Because you didn't think I would have a date?" I asked.

"No, because you didn't know." She giggled behind her hand again.

"Know what?" I asked.

I could just make out the surprise on her face in the moonlight, and she said, "Oh, you *still* don't know?" She giggled behind her hand again. "Well, I'll have to tell you. When you have a date, you are supposed to *shmunzle*."

I sat there stunned. I knew young people did *shmunzle*, but I didn't know they were *expected* to. I was thinking, I couldn't have hugged or kissed Gid. I had no romantic feelings for him at all. Lizzie was still giggling into her hand like a schoolgirl. Then I wondered how Lizzie knew whether we had *shmunzled* or not. I knew I hadn't told her, so that must mean Gid had told someone and she found out. I wondered how many other people knew. I was embarrassed. I excused myself and found the outhouse, where I could be alone.

Later that night, I found out Lizzie had already dated Gid twice. Her third date with him happened that night. Several weeks later, she and Gid started going steady.

My second date introduced me to the world of *shmunzling*. We had both been invited to the same house for overnight. James's kisses were sweet and passionate, and for several nights after that, I longed for his arms around me, and the feel of his lips on mine. Several weeks later, Bishop Dan Wengerd's son, Owen, took me aside and set me up with James for another date for the following Saturday night. Owen said James would come to my house.

On Saturday night, I got dressed in my light green nightdress and waited in my room for hours. James never showed up. I wondered if Owen had set it up without being asked by James, to make it look like I had been stood up.

Owen and I had been in the same class in school. He teased me and made fun of me in seventh and eighth grade. I mostly ignored him, but I used to wonder why he had it in for me. I had never done anything to him. I would never know whether it was James's or Owen's doing that left me feeling alone on that long Saturday night. Around three in the morning, I got under the covers and slept.

The dates I had after that were disgusting. One boy's teeth got in the way when we kissed, another boy's feet smelled so bad I could hardly breathe, and some of the others didn't know where to stop, even though I pushed their hands away. They would come right back as though they didn't understand, or as if they thought I was playing a game with them. I learned the cure for that. It worked for every one of them. I would say, *"Du net!"* (Do not!) and push their hands away. They all had the same reaction. They turned their backs immediately and went to sleep. Then I had to wait until they would slip out in the dark morning hours. I would pretend I was sleeping to save us both from the embarrassment.

One boy complained all the way home about how far it was to my house. By the time he got into my bedroom, I was feeling so guilty for the distance he had traveled, I thought I needed to allow him to do almost anything, short of going all the way. He was the first to break my below-the-waist barrier. I found out the next day, he was one of my second cousins. It's a good thing I didn't like any of the boys I dated, because most of them turned out to be my second cousins. Joe was going steady with Emma at that point. They were second cousins in three different ways, which I found repulsive. I was determined that if I was going to get married, I was not going to marry any relatives. I realized how hard that would be, given that I was related to so many in my community.

I OPENED MY EYES when David pulled into a rest stop somewhere in New York State. He asked, "Can you drive for a while? I am going to need to drive another three hours after I drop you off in Massachusetts."

"Sure, I don't mind driving, but don't you and Tim want to stay overnight at Green Street?"

"No, I told you, I want to get home. I have to go to work tomorrow."

Tim asked, "Dad, can I drive part of the way home?"

"Sure," David said.

After the rest stop, David fell asleep, and Tim put on his headphones to listen to music. I was once more alone with my thoughts, as I cruised along on Route 90. I remembered the days when Joe was the most insufferable, just before he got married and left home.

Traditionally, wedding plans are kept secret within the Amish community until the bishop in the bride's church district announces the wedding that will take place on a Thursday, eleven days later. Thursday is the traditional day for Amish weddings. The announcement at church is what the Amish call "publishing" the wedding. Joe and Emma were published to be married the summer I turned eighteen. Until then, I had thought at least the families of the bride and groom knew of the wedding plans in advance, but Joe and Emma's plans came as a total surprise to me. Mem only smiled when I asked her if she had known about their plans.

During his last few hours at home, Joe bossed us around more than ever. We had to pack his clothes. He would stay at Emma's house during the last eleven days before the wedding day, to help with preparations, like going by buggy to invite people to attend the service, and moving furniture out of the house so the benches could be brought in.

When Mem told me to go upstairs and start his packing, I asked her, "Where are they going to live when they get married?"

"In the basement of Emma's brother's house," Mem said.

I almost danced up the stairs. Sometimes young married couples will live with one set of parents or the other while they get their own place established. I was so relieved that they were not going to live with us.

I took clothes from Joe's drawer and packed them into his suitcase. Downstairs, Joe was bossing Susan to get his bath water ready, right now. I wanted to go down and ask him, "Are you going to treat Emma this way too?" But I told myself, *He is leaving; it doesn't matter anymore.* I knew he was just making sure we knew who was boss, for just as long as he could.

An hour later, when Joe stepped onto his buggy and took off out the driveway, his horse's head reined higher than ever, I got butterflies in my stomach. I dared not show my elation about the fact that he was no longer going to be living at home. I saw Mem looking out the window, and I realized this was very different for her than it was for me. Her eldest son and closest companion was leaving home. I retreated to my room. As I walked past the mirror, I realized I was no longer suppressing the smile that I felt inside. The only time I could catch myself smiling in the mirror was accidentally. Otherwise my smile looked unnatural. For the first time, I saw myself as someone else might see me. I had never thought of myself as attractive before, but I knew if I were looking at someone else, I would think she was pretty—a narrow face with fine features, including a small forehead, a little pug nose that was so characteristic of Mem's side of the family, fair skin with pink cheeks, dark hair and eyes, and plump red lips. When I first read *Snow White* as a child, I thought, *Why would she be pretty? She sounds like she looks like me.*

I lay down on the bed to read, but I couldn't concentrate. I could only think about how my life had just changed. Would the trouble with Datt's violence change, now that Joe was out of the house? Who would Joe ask to be his *neva hocka* (witness) at his wedding? He didn't get along with Lizzie, but usually the oldest unmarried sibling was asked.

The next day, Joe and Emma drove in the lane. They stayed on the buggy and asked Mem if she would send me out. When I came out, Joe said, "Emma and I were wondering if you would be our *neva hocka.*" In Amish, the siblings and their partners are called *neva hocka*—literally, "one who sits beside"—and are the equivalent of a best man and maid of honor, with partners. Usually the sibling chooses who she or he wants for a partner, and the two couples of *neva hocka* have a date the night before and the night of the wedding.

I knew why Joe wasn't asking Lizzie. Part of me wanted to refuse, knowing how much it would hurt her if I accepted, but another part of me wanted the honor, and the chance, finally, to be able to choose my own date. This would be my chance to get to know the person before going to bed with him, like I'd always wanted to. I used to fantasize what it would be like to have someone ask me out on a real date—to eat dinner together and get to know one another—before going to bed with one another. My heart beat faster when I went down my mental list of who I might ask.

"Sure," I said. "I'll do it."

"We thought we would ask Emma's cousin, Albert, to be your partner," Joe said. Emma sat wordlessly by his side.

My excitement melted. I said, "Well, I don't know him."

"That doesn't matter. Emma has chosen her sister Ada to be *neva hocka*, and Ada doesn't know Cousin Andy either, but she is still having him for her partner," Joe said.

My heart sank for Ada. Cousin Andy was like Joe, except with red hair instead of brown. They had gotten in trouble in Pennsylvania for shooting deer out of season, and Andy could undress a woman with his eyes, just like Joe could.

I wanted to say, *So it doesn't matter who I end up in bed with; it can be any stranger?* Instead I said, "Usually people get to choose."

"Did you have someone in mind?" he asked.

I recognized Joe's trap. He was only curious about who I would ask. Even if I named my choices, he would still make me go with Albert, whoever he was. I decided not to give Joe the satisfaction.

"I'd have to think about it," I said. "Yesterday morning I didn't even know you were getting married. I didn't know you wanted me to be *neva hocka* until now."

"You don't have to if you don't want to. Most people would jump at the chance."

"I told you I will do it," I said.

"With Albert?"

I thought about saying no, not with Albert, but I decided the least I could do was deprive him of knowing my secrets.

"Yes," I said. *Since you aren't giving me a choice*, I wanted to add, but I didn't. I hated so much that Joe could still use his power over me.

"Here is a sample of the material for your dress," Emma said, speaking for the first time. She handed me a piece of royal blue polyester. "You can buy it at Spector's."

I took the sample. Usually the bride paid for the dresses of the girls in her wedding. Probably Joe had forbidden it. I doubted Mem would pay for it, either. Usually I had to buy my own dress material with the five dollars weekly allowance I was allowed to keep from the money I made cleaning houses. I could just hear her argument: "But it *will* be your dress."

But Mem surprised me. I had to buy the dress material, but she paid for the organdy material for my cape and apron and for the new white head covering Aunt Saloma made for me. Several days later, while I sewed my dress, I wondered what Albert was like. When I had talked to Emma alone after Joe had gone into the barn to see Datt, she had told me that he was shy and I would be his first date, but that was all I knew. I wished again that I could make my own choice. Still, I looked forward to the wedding. Usually when there was a gathering, I was just one person in the crowd. This would be a chance for me to be noticed.

On the night before the wedding, I pressed my dress and cape and apron and put my new white head covering in a box, ready to go. Joe had sent word that Albert lived too far away and wouldn't be able to pick me up, so I should find my own way to Emma's house. That meant I had to pay for a taxi.

I arrived just before suppertime at Emma's house. Joe met me on the side porch. He had dark stubble on his face. Now that he was getting married, he had to grow a man's beard. Ever since he joined church, he had been growing a little beard, just on his chin. "You're a little early, but you can help out," he said in greeting.

I nodded. "I got word that I should find my own way here, but I didn't know what time I should come."

"Just so you know," Joe said, his voice lowering, "Albert is really shy. Don't embarrass him by talking too much." Then he gave a knowing smile, flashing his crooked teeth, and went inside.

Emma's sister Ada came out to the porch a moment later. "Lomie! Come on in. You don't have to stay out here by yourself!"

I pulled myself together. "What can I help you with?" I asked.

"We're just putting supper on the table." I followed her inside.

In the kitchen, Emma's mother looked up but didn't say hello. I was used to that. I had spent many Sunday afternoons at Emma's, to visit with her sisters, Ada and Ella, before we all went out to singings together. I had once told Joe I didn't think Emma's mother liked me, and Joe had told me that Emma's mother wasn't really as unfriendly as she looked. She was just shy and uneasy around people.

Ada's partner, my Cousin Andy, was there, and so was a young man of slight build with blond hair. The expression in his eyes was telling everyone how much he didn't want to be there. He held his hands on his lap, as though he felt helpless in this situation. I knew he must be Albert. He sat so quietly, I wondered if he thought people wouldn't notice him if he didn't move. I also wondered how he was going to survive the next day, when over two hundred people would notice him.

At supper, we were told what we needed to do the next day. Joe said, "Saloma, you just need to help with whatever Ada is doing." I knew Joe was really telling me I should stay in my place, second to Ada. I nodded agreement.

When I got to the upstairs bedroom that I would share with Albert, he was already sitting on the edge of the bed. I got in on the other side, closest to the wall. Albert blew out the oil lamp and lay down.

We lay there in the dark for a long time. Finally, I said, "Tomorrow will be a different day for all of us."

He was quiet so long that I realized he wasn't going to answer. I wondered what to say next. Should I initiate *shmunzling*, since this was his first date and he wasn't making any moves? Or would that be too forward? Maybe he felt the way I had on my first date.

Albert lay on his stomach. I moved over towards him and put my arm across his back.

He stiffened.

I moved away. Still wondering what I should do next, I heard his breathing suddenly deepen, as though he had fallen asleep. I fell asleep, too.

Albert was not in bed when I awoke in the morning. I got up, dressed in my everyday clothes, and went down for breakfast. I hardly noticed that the October morning had dawned bright and sunny.

After we'd eaten, Emma, Ada, and I dressed in our new bright blue dresses and crisp capes and aprons. Amish women usually get married in blue dresses with white capes and aprons made for the wedding. We had to wear our black head coverings, as if we were going to church for the service, and then we would wear our white coverings for the reception. It was customary for the married women to wear white coverings and the unmarried women to wear black for church services and weddings. This would be Emma's last time wearing her black covering.

When we were dressed, we joined the three men in the wedding party in a room in the basement, next to the washhouse. Through a small window, we could see people arriving by horse and buggy. Many people looked in the window at us. It was usually a secret until the day of the wedding who would be the partner *neva hocka* with the siblings of the bride and groom. I wanted to see surprise register on their faces, but I didn't see any. Rueben's Ada, who had picked raspberries with me at Robert's fruit farm when we were eleven years old, and who had a way of making me feel as though she was superior, looked in at us, and then she chewed her gum and looked the other way, as if this was no big deal.

The wedding would start at nine-thirty in the morning, the same as a church service. I clicked my fingernails together in my nervousness, until Joe told me to stop.

We waited until the singing began out in the barn, slow and long syllables in the traditional Amish chant. Joe led the way. The six of us filed in and stood in front of the chairs provided for us. Mem was not at the service. She was one of the main cooks, so she would come in later to see Joe and Emma exchange their vows.

Datt sat with the middle-aged men, looking meek and mild.

When the six of us were standing in front of our chairs, we sat down in unison. The bishops and ministers got up and shook hands with people and filed out to go to their designated room in the house. After a few minutes, Joe and Emma stood up, and Emma followed Joe humbly into the house to meet with the bishops and ministers for their marriage instructions.

The singing continued with the "Loblied" as the second hymn. When the third hymn had begun, Joe and Emma came back and sat down again. The bishops and ministers returned a few moments later and joined in singing the last verse of the hymn. Then the preaching began. A minister from Emma's church district preached the first sermon. It was very much like a sermon at church, except that it focused on marriage and how the woman should be submissive to her husband. I groaned inwardly and thought to myself that he shouldn't encourage Joe.

There was a break during scripture reading, the same as for a church service. Then Bishop Dan Wengerd stood up and began his sermon. He had been ordained as bishop in our church district the previous year, and this would be the first marriage he would perform. His nervousness was obvious through his pauses and his uneven, jerky movements.

Dan's sermon was shorter than most second sermons are, and then he asked Joe and Emma to step up to him. All the cooks and table waiters had filed into the barn to watch the exchanging of the vows.

I was hoping Bishop Dan wasn't going to mess this up. I wanted to make sure they were really married. I watched as they repeated their pledges after Bishop Dan, and then Bishop Dan joined their hands and pronounced them man and wife.

Joe and Emma looked as nervous as Bishop Dan, and I wondered if it was catching. Emma certainly seemed as submissive as a woman could ever become as she walked towards her seat, behind Joe.

The cooks and table waiters went back to their work in the kitchen. The congregation knelt, and Bishop Dan read a long German prayer. I couldn't help but feel relieved that my life had changed for the better. At the same time, as I looked at Emma, kneeling so quietly next to me, face so unreadable, I felt an ache of sympathy. She was now at the mercy of Joe and bound to him in ways that no one ever had been before. I said a prayer asking for God to have mercy on Emma.

After we stood for a scripture reading, we sat down, and people began to sing a lively hymn. When the last notes died away, all was quiet. The six of us stood up and filed out before the rest of the congregation.

Emma, Ada, and I quickly went upstairs and replaced our black coverings with our white ones. Emma was quiet, only asking Ada about where she had put this or that. It seemed impossible to me that someone could think about such small details right after such a huge change had been made in her life.

Several minutes later, we sat at the bridal corner, or *eck*, in the living room, with our respective partners. The men filed in and sat on one side of the table, and the women sat on the other side. When the bishop gave the signal, everyone bowed their heads for silent prayer, and then big platters and bowls of food were brought to the table by the table waiters.

Lizzie and Ella waited on our table. Lizzie was trying her best to do what she was supposed to, but Joe managed to get a dig in under his breath, something about Ella doing most of the work. They brought the six of us the choicest chicken and special dishes, homemade bread with apple butter, heaps of mashed potatoes and bowls of gravy, dressing, coleslaw, fresh garden peas, and applesauce. Ella's face was flushed red with the warmth of the day and the effort she was exerting to do her job just right. Lizzie looked as flushed as Ella did. Sarah and Susan, the next most honored table waiters, served the tables right next to the *eck*.

For dessert, we had strawberry tapioca pudding, vanilla pudding, apple, cherry, blueberry, and strawberry pies. The six of us had a special strawberry pie that had a whipped cream topping and had been chilled in the icebox. Halfway through the dessert, the men who were married to the cooks came around to collect money for the cooks and table waiters. They shook their saucepans vigorously, making the coins rattle loudly as people tossed money into them.

After the meal was done, Joe and Emma visited with folks out under the shade of the maple tree in the front yard while Ada and I gathered all the presents into one upstairs bedroom. The sound of the spirited hymns drifted up from the living room, where the men sat around the now empty tables. There had been a second sitting after we left the table. At least at weddings men and women ate together, rather than the men first and women last, as was done at family gatherings. The table waiters cleared the tables, washed the dishes, and reset the tables again for the evening meal.

After about an hour, Joe went off to the barn with the menfolk to give out cigars. I could tell by his stride that he was feeling like "king shit of the manure pile," the way he often referred to others who he thought were "getting too big for their britches."

Emma came upstairs to her bedroom and unwrapped presents: bowls of glass, plastic, and stainless steel; platters, pitchers, glasses, dishpans and a drainer; pots and pans; bath and dish towels, sheets, tablecloths, and potholders; a gas iron and a lantern; and every imaginable household item. Ada and I took turns recording who had given what gifts in Emma's wedding album. Women and girls came in small groups to watch; then they would drift away and another group would come in. The room got warm and stuffy, and cigar smoke drifted up from downstairs.

I took a break and went out in the cool shade when it was Ada's turn to record. Sitting beneath the huge maple in the front yard, I closed my eyes and listened to the sounds of talking and laughter, of the horses moving quietly where they grazed in the field nearby, and an occasional car driving by on the road. I could smell the meatloaf baking, along with something sweet, probably date pudding. Enveloped by the very air of the Amish around me, I longed to just be able to give in, to accept that this life that I had been born into was the one meant for me. To know that sometime in the next five years, I would be in Emma's place, unwrapping wedding presents, and my new husband would right now be out in the barn, being congratulated by his friends. I imagined we would go home to our own place, and soon I would have children of my own.

I was brought out of my reverie when I heard a group of women approaching the bench where I was sitting. They brought out benches from inside to join me in the shade beneath the maple. I swallowed down my feelings. Aunts and cousins came by and visited in between their duties in the kitchen. Lizzie and Ella sat there for a while. They looked tired. Sarah and Susan were taking their turn in the kitchen.

The crowd thinned out in the late afternoon. Some people went home for chores with plans to come back for the evening festivities. Others left for the day. Just before supper was served to the married folks, the young people started arriving. They gathered in upstairs bedrooms with the girls in one room, the boys in another.

Joe began lining up the young folks to go downstairs. He had them line up boy, girl. He didn't give much thought about who ended up with whom. The young men resisted and went back into the bedroom, feigning shyness. Joe told them if they didn't want to eat, they could stay in the room, and they stopped resisting. Joe used to resist this lineup even more than other young men, and suddenly he was in charge of getting them to behave.

Finally, when all the young folks were lined up with Joe and Emma in the lead, we went to our place at the corner of the table again. This time we had meatloaf, buttered noodles, several kinds of slaw, corn relish, applesauce, vanilla pudding, fruit pies, and the date pudding I'd smelled earlier. The money rattlers came back with their saucepans and gathered more money.

After the second sitting of supper was over, men carried lanterns to the barn and the dancing began. Someone turned on a tape recorder, and in the lantern light, the "party playing" began. Joe and Emma danced together for the last time. Once their wedding day had passed, it was forbidden for couples to dance. This was because when one joined the church, one was expected to obey the rules of the church, yet the elders still didn't fully enforce all the rules until young people got married. Marriage was considered the last step into adulthood, and therefore the expectations for full membership and the upholding of all the church rules now applied. Dancing or "party playing" was considered a courtship ritual and therefore superfluous for married couples.

I danced with Ada, but no young men cut in to dance with me. I didn't even see Albert.

It was well after midnight before the lanterns were taken from the barn—the signal for the young folks to go home. Couples got into buggies and drove off. Dates often took place the night of weddings.

Joe took me to the side of the barn. I knew he wasn't setting up a date for me, because I already had mine. He said, "You can sleep in the same room you slept in last night, but Albert won't be coming in. He decided he wanted to sleep alone tonight. I just thought I would let you know."

Before I could say anything, Joe walked across the yard toward the house and left me standing there. I watched his retreating back disappear into the darkness, the light of the lantern he was carrying casting moving shadows that crisscrossed the yard with each determined step he took. I felt so rejected and alone, I wanted to cry—and then I realized that was exactly what Joe wanted me to feel. He had used his own wedding to "bring me down a notch," as he often phrased it—as an excuse to dominate us. As if every woman would get too confident of herself if she didn't have a male reminding her every now and again who's boss. *Unless I am just a reject and everyone knows it except me,* I thought. I went to bed feeling more alone than ever. Even the darkness in the room was oppressive. I lay awake a long time before I finally drifted into a sleep that did not refresh me.

I awoke to the sound of others in the house moving about. It was my duty to help with cleaning up. I forced my body out of bed. Did Emma's sisters and parents know that I had slept alone? It would be just like Joe to tell them, to embarrass me even more. It was also like him to leave that to my imagination, so that I would keep wondering.

Joe and Emma were in the kitchen, among all the dirty dishes left from the night before. Joe's hooded eyes looked bleary. I couldn't read his expression. I wondered if his night with Emma had been different than any other night he'd spent with her in the last year. I decided I didn't want to know. I looked at Albert, who looked as though he was trying to disappear down a hole. I decided I was done feeling sorry for him that he was so shy.

We all had to do dishes right after breakfast. All the ones from the previous night were waiting, piled high on every countertop and table in the kitchen. I had never seen so many dirty dishes in my life. Emma's mother set up each of us three couples at different tables with wash and rinse water. I wondered when this tradition had started, with men helping with the dishes only after a wedding. I had not seen Joe do dishes since he was about twelve.

Albert went through the motions of drying, but he clearly didn't know how to do it. I could have wiped three glasses by the time he did one. I wondered why Joe hadn't excused him from doing dishes with me, after the embarrassment of not having been together for a date the night before. I wished I had the nerve to ask him why he had bothered to say yes to being one of the *neva hocka* at all. I wanted to ask him if he thought being shy was worse than feeling rejected. And I wanted to tell him I wouldn't have chosen him, but Joe and Emma didn't give me the choice, and did he know that he spoiled my day with his shyness, and how he might as well not have been there?

I finished washing our mountain of dishes; then I called a taxi from the phone booth down the road and went home. Mem mercifully let me go to bed and sleep, even though it was the middle of the day.

When I awoke late in the afternoon, Mem warned me that I wouldn't be able to sleep through the night, but I did. Sleep helped to soften the memories of the disappointment, hurt, and confusion of Joe's wedding.

Mem with an "English" friend. This photo was taken while she was working for Grace Bradley's family before she was married.

In this photo, Joey, Lizzie, and two neighbor children are playing in a galvanized bathtub in our neighbors' yard. This is the same bathtub we set up next to the woodstove in our living room in the wintertime.

Three sisters playing in the neighbors' yard in June 1963. From left to right: me, Susan, and Lizzie.

Siblings playing in the neighbors' yard in June 1963. From left to right: me, Joey, Lizzie, sister Susan, and neighbor Brian.

Playing in the daffodils: me (standing), Lizzie, Joey, and neighbor Brian.

I was the lone Amish girl in the class in kindergarten at East Claridon Public School in 1962.

Joey (on the left) and me (on the right) at a birthday picnic in the neighbors' yard.

We were just out of Mem's view from the living room window when our friends' mother took this picture of us, waiting for the bus on my first day of kindergarten: neighbor Susan, Lizzie, neighbor Brian, Joey, and me.

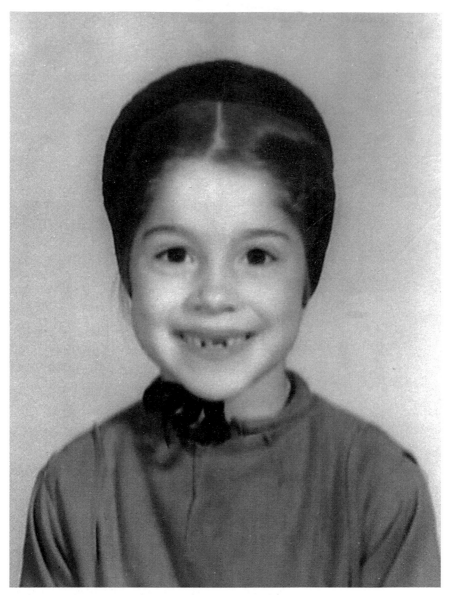

Me in second grade. At school on picture day, my teacher said I could stay in the classroom, because she was told Amish children don't have their pictures taken, but I popped up out of my seat and said, "Oh, but my Mom said I could be in the class picture!" I got in line with the other children, and when it was my turn to have an individual photo taken, I sat up on the stool and smiled unabashedly into the lights and camera. Years later I found a tiny photo with my school records; I borrowed it and had it enlarged.

I was taking care of Scotty once a week while I cleaned for his parents. His mother took this picture of us. I was twenty years old.

My sisters and I had a camera on the sly when my nephew was a baby. One of them took this photo of me holding him. Baby boys wore dresses until they were out of diapers in my community.

I call this photo "screening Mem"; a sibling snuck this shot of her through a screen from an upstairs window.

A picturesque Amish farm near Walnut Creek, Ohio.

This is a typical Amish cluster of buildings—what I call a farmette. Each of these buildings has at least one distinct function. Amish homes need at least one outbuilding for storing buggies and housing horses, as well as pasturing land. A larger cluster of buildings is common on income-generating farms.

Note the corn crib with the round, metal roof. Another common element on an Amish homestead is at least one tree to provide shade from the summer heat.

When I was a child, this type of windmill was commonly used for pumping water. Nowadays most families have motorized pumps.

David and me by Lake Thun in Switzerland—one of the most beautiful places on earth. This is in the region where the Swiss Brethren, ancestors to the Amish, formed their beliefs.

Four sisters and Aunt Martha at a family get together: Susan, Lizzie (who sadly was suffering from cancer), me, Aunt Martha (who looks like a smaller version of Mem), and Sarah.

Me at Amherst College in 2010.

And when he had given thanks, he broke it, and said, Take, eat: this is my body,
which is broken for you: do this in remembrance of me.

1 CORINTHIANS 11:24

A Grain by the Wayside

T im shifted in his seat and asked how soon we would get to Northampton. I told him we were almost in Albany, and that we still had a few
hours to go. David awoke and said he would continue to drive whenever
I was ready. After another stop at a rest area, we settled into the positions most
comfortable for all of us—David driving, me in the front passenger seat, and
Tim listening to music in the back seat.

My thoughts drifted back to the events in the days before I left the community, particularly my struggles around becoming a member of the church.
The choice that many people, looking in from the outside, think Amish young
people have about whether they leave or stay in the community is a myth, at
least in my experience. I certainly did not feel like I had a choice. It was as if I
was being led down a long corridor, in which there was light ahead of me and
darkness behind me, with someone representing the church firmly guiding me
down that corridor in the direction of "joining church." To choose not to join,
I would have had to wrench my elbow away from that someone, and run back
into the darkness of the unknown. I lacked the courage to face the unknown,
but I also lacked the necessary conviction to be baptized into the church. I
followed the firm hand at my elbow because it was the easiest thing to do.

First came subtle hints, then outright suggestions, and finally admonish-
ments that I should "join church" and be baptized the summer I was turning

nineteen. I was unsure about becoming an official member because I questioned my ability to be a "good member" of the church. A "good" member is one who does not question the ways of the Amish. I knew that if I did join the church and then left, I would be shunned for the rest of my life. But I would not be shunned if I hadn't yet become a member.

I had some good reasons for joining. I wanted to be more accepted in the community. I thought I would finally get answers to the questions about Amish ways that I kept asking. There were also the reasons for joining that I was not admitting to myself. I secretly hoped that if I became an upstanding church member, people would reach out and help me. People in the community were aware of the difficulties we had in our family. I was still nurturing a fantasy that someone like Olin Clara would step forward and offer to take me into her home, despite my rebellious reputation. I wondered why no one realized I was only rebelling against the situation I had to live in. I told myself that if only I didn't have to live in this family situation, I could be as good an Amish person as anyone. I thought, maybe if I became an obedient member of the church, it would be easier for Olin and Clara Yoder to invite me to come live with them.

It seemed to me that Olin Clara was the only person in the church community who cared about me. She was short, energetic, talkative, and could make anyone who walked into her home feel welcome. She seemed younger than Mem, even though she was four years older. She was also the best pie baker in the community.

When I was nine years old, she asked Mem if I could come and help her with cleaning and baking on Saturdays. I used to wonder why she would ask me to help her, out of all the girls in the community, but as I got older, I realized that she was really helping me out. She was showing me what was normal in other families, something to strive for when I started my own family someday. I hadn't dared to let myself think she was doing it just because she liked me and enjoyed my company. My mind drifted back to my first memories of Olin Clara, when I was four years old and she was the only person who accepted my outgoing ways.

An "English" family used to give us second-hand items that they had collected in their church. A red pair of boots in just my size arrived in one of the boxes. Mem didn't intend on letting me wear them, because Amish weren't allowed to wear red, but when Sunday morning came and she didn't have any other boots that fit me, she wriggled them on over my shoes and said, "Now when we get to church, we will need to hide these in the corner of the washhouse."

I nodded, and then we bundled up in black coats, scarves, bonnets, and capes, and huddled under three buggy blankets for the long, cold ride. Under Mem's feet in a denim bag was the soapstone that she had warmed on the wood stove all night. Joe, Lizzie, and I sat in the back seat. Lizzie and I wrapped the buggy blankets around our legs and feet. I wished I didn't have to cover those red boots.

Church was at the Eli Yoders' house that day. They lived the farthest away of the people in our church district. I asked how far we had to go, and Mem said five miles. By the time Datt stopped the buggy at the washhouse door, I had decided that five miles was a very long way. When we walked into the washhouse, I saw Olin Clara looking at me. She always had a smile and a kind word for me. I walked up to where she stood with a group of women and girls, ready to go into the warm kitchen. I held up one foot and said, "Look at my boots. I have new boots!"

Everyone became so silent, I could hear myself breathe. I put my foot down and looked at Mem. Her face was flushed with shame. I looked at Olin Clara, and she smiled at me reassuringly. Mem pulled me over to the side of the washhouse and said, "Take those off!" She pulled them off me so quickly that my shoes came off, too. "I told you not to show these to anyone!"

I was embarrassed for doing something wrong, but Olin Clara chatted pleasantly with Mem and me, and she said quietly, "Don't worry about it." I could feel Mem's hold on my hand relax.

I wore the red boots home from church that day, and then they disappeared.

YEARS LATER, OLIN CLARA rescued me from shame in a different church service. On the bright, sunny morning of my ninth birthday, I awoke feeling excited about going to church. I knew people in church wouldn't sing Happy Birthday, but maybe if I told a few people, they would at least wish me a happy one. Church seemed extra long that day, but eventually it ended, like all other church services.

I ran through the yard and into the house. Al Ada's spotless house gleamed. A patch of sunlight from the porch window came through the door to the living room and fell onto the hardwood floor and woven rug. I smelled coffee and baloney.

"It's my birthday," I said to the woman with the baby, who was putting soup in a bowl to feed him.

She looked at me for a moment in silence, and then turned away.

"Today's my birthday," I said to the woman next to her.

She turned away and pretended she hadn't heard, looking embarrassed.

"It's my birthday," I said to my friend Ruth's mother, who was pouring coffee.

"How old are you?" she asked in an uninterested voice.

"Nine," I said, but she had already turned to talk to someone else. Women turned their reproachful eyes on me, and I wondered what was wrong with telling people it was my birthday.

My face hot, I turned and went back out to the shed. Olin Clara was helping to put plates of bread, baloney, pickles, butter, and bowls of peanut butter onto the long tables. She was slim and short, with a sprightly spring to her walk. And she stopped, looked at me, and said, "Happy Birthday! Aren't you turning nine today?"

I nodded and picked up two plates of baloney and followed her to the table. I looked at the back of her white organdy cape with the two neat pleats and wondered why everyone was not as kind as Olin Clara.

A few days later, a birthday card came in the mail for me. In it was a bookmark that Olin Clara had made. She had drawn morning glories in a vine around the border and had written "Happy Birthday, Saloma" in the middle, in her beautiful handwriting. She used clear contact paper to cover the bookmark. I was touched to know Clara had made it for me and awed that she could make something so beautiful.

I hung the bookmark on the corner shelf in my bedroom that held the pretty dishes I had gotten for my birthdays.

The Sunday afternoon after church on my ninth birthday, as I was popping corn, Mem asked, "Lomie, how would you like to go and help Olin Clara with her cleaning next Saturday?"

Mem had a soft expression in her light blue eyes. I was surprised about what she had just said, and also by the way she was looking at me. I didn't know what to say.

"Olin Clara asked me today if I could spare you, and I said yes. She is particular and you would have to do a good job, but I think you can do it."

"Do you think so? Why didn't she ask one of the older girls in the community?"

"I think she asked you because she wanted you," Mem said.

The next Saturday, I started out on the mile-long walk to Olin Clara's house. The shadows were still long, and the dew sparkled on the tips of the blades of grass, points of light under the morning sun. Red-winged blackbirds sang in the fields along the way. I wondered how they could make the sound of chirping and ringing at the same time. I spotted a redheaded woodpecker on a large beech tree in the woods. The sun shone on his bright red head and his black and white wing feathers as he hammered away at the hole in the beech tree, so fast his head was a blur. I stood still and watched him until he flew in his distinctive dips into the woods and out of sight.

When I walked past the Gingerich farm, I waved to Sara Mae, who was hanging out clothes. She and I were almost twins. She was born the day before me, at the same place where I was born. There was an Amish woman who used to be a midwife, who had people come to her house to have babies. Mem and Ada had ended up there together, each bearing a baby daughter. I was Mem's third child, and Sara Mae was Ada's fourth child. Ada had seventeen children altogether in subsequent years, and Mem had seven.

After I waved to Sara Mae, I kept walking up the strip of narrow paved road, up the last hill to Olin Clara's house. Her garden was on the hillside below the house, with vegetables coming up in different shades of green, bordered by flowers of all colors. Next to the garden was a bird feeder attracting chickadees, nuthatches, titmice, and goldfinches.

In front of Clara's house was the biggest maple tree I had ever seen, with its gnarled branches reaching out like twisted arms, spreading their leaves out across the yard. Four of us once tried holding hands around it and we couldn't reach all the way around.

As I walked up the sidewalk leading to the kitchen door, a tabby cat walked up and meowed and rubbed against my leg. As I petted her, she arched her back against my hand. I knocked at the door. The smell of freshly baked cookies and pies wafted through the screen door.

Clara said, "Come in, Salomi," in a pleasant voice. She was the only person who called me that, combining my Amish name with my English one. I decided I liked it.

I stepped into the kitchen, and Clara pulled out a kitchen chair and said, "Have a seat. I'm sure you are tired after your walk. Do you like butterscotch chip cookies? Can I get you something to drink? I have lemonade or milk."

"Oh, I came to do work; you don't need to feed me first thing," I said.

She nodded her head and said, "Just sit down," as she patted the back of the chair. I did. The cookies were warm, sweet, and crumbly. I finished the glass of milk and got up to wash my glass and plate at the kitchen sink with the chrome faucet. It felt like magic to be able to get hot or cold water just by turning one of the knobs.

I continued to go to Olin Clara's house on Saturdays for several years. I learned her methods of baking pies and cookies, and I learned through her appreciation of my mother's homemade bread that Mem made the best bread in the community. I had assumed every mem in the community made bread like hers, but once when I brought a fresh loaf to Clara, she praised Mem's bread so highly and in such a sincere way that I began to realize Mem's bread was indeed a specialty. That day when I got home and told Mem how much Clara liked her bread, her face turned pink, and she said, "Oh, she is just saying that to make you feel good." But I could tell she was pleased as she tried to suppress a smile.

Mem did not often get compliments from other Amish people. First of all, compliments were not given as freely as in mainstream American culture, because the belief in the community is that people should be humble. But Mem's situation was more complicated than that. I came to understand later that somehow she was a threat to many other women in the community, especially the bishop's wife. They did not want Mem, who was married to "Sim" after all, to be better respected than they were. Olin Clara did not seem to be motivated by these same sentiments. Later in life, she became Mem's one true friend in the church district, after my sisters and I had all left the community.

When I was done with eighth grade, I began cleaning the homes of "English" people, and I drifted away from Olin Clara, though I always knew she was there. And so, as I struggled with whether or not to join church, I hoped Olin Clara would grasp how difficult my life had become. I wanted to believe that I could be a better person if my life were more bearable. I only dimly understood that Olin Clara could never do what I wished for. She would be ostracized in the community for undermining my parents and the church. She had smiled at me one Sunday and asked me if I was planning on joining church. I said I didn't know yet. She said, "I hope you do." I felt that she genuinely wanted me to be a fellow church member with her, and it made me feel welcome. Because she was really the only person I wanted to please, I thought about doing it for her. Then I felt guilty, because I knew I should be doing it for my own good, and in the name of Jesus. While I think on some level I understood my resistance, it was not until much later that I understood the nature of this struggle. I wanted to walk a spiritual path that allowed for asking fundamental questions, and I did not want to be instructed on what to believe, especially in matters of the soul. At the time I only knew what I didn't want, but I had not yet figured out what I *did* want. The people pressuring me, such as Brother Joe, took advantage of my ambivalence.

We visited Joe and Emma one day soon after their first baby was born. I was quieter than usual that day, observing what was happening around me. Joe and Emma seemed so happy together, living in the basement of Emma's brother Melvin and his family's house. I wondered if Joe still called folks who lived in basements "groundhogs." Then I realized I was jealous of him. He had made a new life for himself, and now he didn't have to put up with Datt. With their sweet little baby, Lester, it seemed to me that Joe and Emma had it all. I put my face next to Lester's and breathed his warm, clean baby scent.

"Just remember, he is not yours," Joe said. He and I were alone in the kitchen for a few moments with the baby, while the others had gone outside to look at the garden.

I smiled at Lester and said, "Okay, I'll keep that in mind."

"Is it any better at home?"

I shrugged, knowing better than to answer that.

He sent me a look from under his drooping eyelids. This was the look he would give when he wanted to convey that we were best friends, and I was supposed to forget all he had done in the past. "Are you going to join church this summer?"

"I am thinking about it."

"I think that would really help."

I didn't know what to say. I wondered if Mem or Datt had asked him to talk to me. I shrugged again. "Maybe it would help. But what if it doesn't?"

"Then at least you would be doing the right thing," Joe said, and then he went outside.

I sighed and turned, blocking the sunlight from the window so that it wouldn't fall on the baby's face. As I watched Joe walking towards the others, I pondered something I'd just seen in his pantry. When I was putting away leftovers from the meal, I saw a bottle of Black Velvet high up on a shelf. I knew this was Joe's favorite brand of whiskey, because he used to keep a bottle of it hidden in the haymow when he was still living at home. If he really believed it was the right thing for me to join church, then why wasn't he adhering to the rules that forbade church members to drink alcohol? Maybe, I thought, life wasn't as perfect for him as it appeared.

I BASICALLY KNEW, in the end, that I didn't have a choice. If I didn't join church that summer, it would have to be the next. In the meantime, people in the community would become more distrustful of me. So, when the morning came to start taking instructions for baptism, I prepared to join church with four other young people. Our first formal instructions began one bright and sunny May morning.

I got to the Gingeriches in time to see Sara Mae and her sister, Elizabeth, finish pinning their capes into place. Both of them were also joining. Then we walked to John Detweilers' for the church service. We waited until after the elders left to go into the house. Then Noah Wengerd, Bishop Dan's son, rose to follow the ministers, and we girls followed him to an upstairs bedroom where the elders had gathered. We sat down on the bench that faced the elders, while each of them took turns talking to us. The ministers quoted many verses from the Bible in High German. We sat and listened. When the bishop asked us to promise to obey the rules of the church, we took turns giving our prescribed yeses. Eventually Bishop Dan asked us to rejoin the service. The ministers stayed for their normal closed-door session during the first part of every church service.

After three weeks of this, I realized that "instruction" just meant that we got our own personal preaching session. There was not going to be any question-and-answer time. I kept my silence and tried to accept what they were saying. We continued to follow this pattern through the summer.

At home, Datt and I had one conflict after another. I had hoped that once

I started joining church, he would stop giving me such a hard time, but I was wrong.

Datt didn't like how late the young people's gatherings, or "singings," started. He kept nagging me to go earlier. I would argue, "But Datt, what am I supposed to do, get there at eight when the singing doesn't start until ten?" As usual, he couldn't be reasoned with. He kept saying that the singings didn't start so late in his day, and on and on. Instead of repeating, "But Datt, I can't help that things have changed," I began to hire the taxi driver for the time Datt wanted me to go. Then I had the driver drop me off at a place close to the singing location. I'd take a walk on the country roads until the singing started.

On one such evening, as I was walking along, enjoying the cool breeze after a hot day of sitting in church, I imagined I was someone else—someone new, who I didn't even know. I tried to walk like an English girl, taking little dainty steps, swishing my skirt, imagining my hair hanging loose to my waist.

Sarah and Susan often mimicked the way I walked. According to them, I always held one arm still and swung the other like a pendulum, and placed my feet heavily on the ground. I knew they were exaggerating my walk when they mocked me, but it had the effect they wanted: I became self-conscious. So, when others mentioned my manner of walking, I took their comments as criticism.

That night, when I turned around to walk back to the singing, still feeling like the "English" girl I wanted to be, I saw two girls a half mile down the road. I walked towards them. When I came close enough to recognize them, I wished I could hide. They were two of my second cousins, Saloma and Lydia, with whom I had never gotten along. As they neared, I remembered a day when I was perhaps seven years old and Mem and I had gone to a quilting at Saloma's mem's house.

Back then, going anywhere with Mem was a treat. On that day, she had driven our old gelding, Don, to the quilting, and he had plodded along, safe and steady, the way he always did. When we got there, I sought out the girls who were my age. I tagged along with them, playing house, kickball, and going for cart-and-pony rides. Then I noticed that whenever I'd look up from playing, the other girls were running off to the barn or to one of the sheds, and I had to go and find them.

After three or four times of doing this, Saloma picked up a red scooter that had been lying beside the driveway and said, "Lomie, look, can you do this?" She used one foot to scoot along.

I said, "Yes," and she handed me the scooter. When I had barely pushed off on the scooter, I heard bare feet stampeding towards the barn. I looked back, dropped the scooter, and caught up to the girls. They walked in front of the stalls, saying, "That's your horse, that is so-and-so's horse," and so on until they stood in front of Don. Saloma said, "Lomie, this is your family's horse."

"How did you know? I asked.

"Because it has such big feet," she scoffed. She and the other girls giggled into their hands. I stood staring at Don's feet while the girls moved away. I knew that Mem and Datt didn't have a real "buggy" horse, but it had never occurred to me to be self-conscious about the size of our horse's feet. I had far more difficult things to worry about.

I didn't run after the girls after that. I didn't care what they did.

Now, seeing Saloma and Lydia approach, I wished I had continued to walk in the other direction. I didn't like Lydia's mousy-looking face with its constant snooty expression. And Saloma could still make me feel inferior, even though we were nineteen, not seven.

When we met, Saloma and Lydia said hello, and I was polite in return. Saloma said, "I was wondering what you were doing on this road."

"How could you tell it was me? I didn't know who you were until just a little way back."

"I could tell who you were by the way you walk," Saloma said.

"Oh." I wished I could have kept the surprise out of my voice. To myself I said, *So much for walking like someone else, never mind being someone else.*

AFTER I STARTED LEAVING for the singings earlier, Datt started telling me I shouldn't dance at the singings if I planned to be baptized. I didn't think he could control that, because Amish young folks had always danced until they got married. Since it wasn't against the church rules, I wasn't going to give it up. It was one of the few things I enjoyed doing. So I ignored him and continued to dance at the singings.

One Sunday during our instruction, Bishop Dan said, "There is a brother in the church who has brought before us the fact that one of you young people continues to dance at the singings. If that person can promise that this will stop, then we can continue." Then he looked at me and waited.

I looked up. "Me?" I asked. I looked at Noah and Sara Mae, the two people who had always preceded me in answering the obedient "yes" to any promises the preachers asked us to make on our conduct as future members of the church. This was the first time Bishop Dan had singled anyone out all summer.

Bishop Dan shuffled his feet nervously and said, "Yes, well, ah, all of you should make the same promise, so Noah, why don't you start?"

There were the five expected yeses. Then Dan continued on. I didn't hear anything he was saying. I was thinking how much I hated Datt. I ground my teeth. I knew that Datt had used the church and Bishop Dan to get his way. I wished I hadn't been blindsided, so that I could think before I made such a promise—because I knew I had to honor it. What, I wondered, would have happened if I had said no? For the next several weeks when I went to the singings, I refrained from dancing. I found it very tempting to join in when I watched the others dancing, but I had made a promise and I felt I had to honor it.

One of Bishop Dan's daughters got married that summer. Out in the barn the night of the wedding, people danced. Noah and all his brothers and sisters danced, along with the other young folks. I joined in too, once I realized I wasn't expected to honor the promise I had made. Dan had probably made us promise to get Datt off his back, and then had forgotten all about it. I thought Bishop Dan was a hypocrite and a coward after that.

I wondered if I should stop taking instructions for baptism. I knew young people who had started and then quit after one or two weeks, because they had decided they weren't ready. That was okay with the community if the person wasn't already nineteen and if it wasn't halfway through the summer. I would be criticized unmercifully if I quit now.

I WAS GETTING READY to be baptized when we heard the news about Mem's father (Dodde). He used to drive his horse and buggy to Uncle Joe's carpenter shop every day to help with the carpentry work. One morning the horse came galloping in, as though he were running away from something. Uncle Joe rushed out, caught him, and found Dodde slumped over on the seat. The moment he touched him, he realized Dodde was dead. Dodde had had a heart attack on the way over. He had lived alone for five years since Momme's death.

Dodde's funeral was probably the biggest one I have ever attended. He had known many people inside and outside the community and was well respected. When it came time for the relatives to file past the coffin, the aunts and cousins stood in a tight cluster and cried, long and loudly. I found myself in the middle of this cluster of perhaps fifty women. I cried quietly into my handkerchief. I wondered whether Dodde was in the good place, and if so, was he there because he had lived a good Amish life? What if he had been the same good person and not been Amish? Would he still be in Heaven?

At the graveyard, when the men were singing the sad tune about meeting in a better land someday, I lifted my eyes to the cottony clouds above us. I felt as if there was a presence in the blue between the clouds. I took a deep breath and let the tears flow. I wanted to know I was doing the right thing by being baptized. I wished I could be a better Amish person. Through my tears, I saw one of the ministers looking at me. I hoped he would think I was crying for Dodde. Then I felt like a liar for thinking that. What would he think if he knew about my inner conflict, when my baptism was only days away?

The night before baptismal services, all five of us who were to be baptized the next day were supposed to meet at the deacon's house. Joe arrived at our house while I was getting ready. Brother Simon had just gone out to fetch water from the pump so I could wash my hair, and he didn't come in for what seemed like a long time.

"Hurry up, Simon!" I shouted out the window. "I'm going to be late!"

Joe said to Mem so that I would hear: "The night before Lomie is baptized, she is like this? Maybe she isn't ready."

I wanted to say, *You are right, Joe, I'm not, so why don't you go explain that to the preachers for me tonight?* But I knew if I showed my anger, he would say something to make things worse.

Later, as I was bending over the hole in the outhouse, throwing up, the way I usually did after I had stuffed myself, I remembered what Joe had said. Maybe he was right. Maybe I wasn't fit to be a member of the church. I wondered if I could back out. If I did, would I be protecting the church from myself, or the other way around?

I continued to prepare to go to the deacon's house because I didn't know what else to do. The purpose of getting together at his house was to read and discuss the German "articles of faith." These articles had been handed down through the generations and pertained to the *Ordnung*, or set of church rules. They also included interpretations of biblical passages that supported the rules of the *Ordnung*. We each chose one of the articles that we would read at the gathering at the deacon's house. I chose the fourth, about how Jesus had been born on earth to atone for the sins of all mankind, from the time of Adam until the end of the world. It seemed to me that this was a universal message of salvation, not just for Amish people being baptized into the church. I had studied my article well. I read the passages from the Bible that were referenced in the article—about Jesus' birth when Mary swaddled him and laid him in a manger, about his crucifixion and how he rose after the third day. My favorite passage was the one about hearing the sound of the wind, but not knowing from where it comes, and so it is with everyone born in the Spirit. I liked the mystery and the universal message of the passage.

We each read our article, then Bishop Dan explained what it meant. By the time I read my article in the presence of the four other young people and the five ministers, I was able to read it with some understanding. When he began to explain the article I had read, he shuffled his feet nervously and said, "Well it means—ah—just the way you read it."

I didn't know whether it was a compliment or not. I thought I detected a begrudging tone in his voice. I was disappointed. I wanted to find out whether I understood it properly. It felt as though I was about to make promises I didn't understand, so I had tried to at least understand the article I was presenting. Wilma Jean, the youngest of us, was reading her article when I realized that I was not expected to understand what I promised. Being *willing* to make whatever promises the church asked was much more important than understanding. It seemed to me that our Anabaptist ancestors who were persecuted or died for their faith, were struggling against a church establishment. At the time it was the Catholic Church and the Reformed Church, with much of the struggle over adult baptism, so that people could actively *choose* salvation. Now adult baptism had become the expectation, a way of certifying the Amish belief system. To follow this unquestioningly, or because one was afraid to do otherwise, seemed to me no different than it would have been for a member of the Catholic Church in Europe going along with the established church out of fear of reprisal. At least that has changed—our ancestors were persecuted for leaving the established church.

The Amish form of banning former members is not an unbearable physical persecution or execution. It is a belief system that a child inherits, in which one believes one is damned if one leaves the Amish. In a society that practices forgiveness in almost every facet of life, the belief is that God is the one and only Judge, and that we as mortal men are in no position to judge another's life. The one exception to this belief is when one leaves the fold—then all hope is lost for that person's salvation. Parents whose small children die are often told, as a "comforting" thought, that at least the child is in heaven. The Amish belief is that it is better to lose a child through death than for that child to grow up and leave the Amish, because then the child is lost "to the world." In such a belief system, no one in the community is harder on a person thinking of leaving the fold than the person herself. This is where I found myself, as I pondered the question of my spiritual path. I surely did not want to lose my soul, never mind the guilt of putting my parents through the agony of losing their daughter "to the world."

Yet the unease of going through the process without my heart being in it did not leave me for a minute. The persecution that our ancestors endured for leaving the established church was physically brutal and absolute. Instilling the belief system in young children is a different kind of reprisal altogether. In this system, the young adult who leaves is robbed of hope in her own salvation. The idea of hell fire is as real to a young adult, who as a child has listened to many fire-and-brimstone sermons, as it must have been for an Anabaptist to hear his or her death sentence being read. I was suddenly aware, as the bishop mumbled on about the article Wilma Jean had read that whether I understood the articles was of little importance. What was required of me to become a respectable member of the church was to lay down my questions and follow obediently, with a willing heart. I brought my attention back to what Bishop Dan was saying about the fifth article: that Jesus had died for all our sins, but it was only those who feel unworthy of his love and forgiveness who can hope to achieve salvation. I decided to humble myself and submit to the expectations of the church.

CHURCH WAS AT THE BISHOP's daughter and her husband's place the day of baptismal services. The service was held in the shed, where the cement floor was cracked, rough, and dirty. During the service, I kept thinking about the five of us who were going to be baptized, kneeling on that floor in our best Sunday clothes. Why hadn't they spread straw on the floor, as people usually did in sheds or barns where they hosted church services? Then I closed my eyes and tried to put such improper thoughts out of my mind.

Bishop Dan preached the second sermon, and then he had everyone stand up. He asked those of us who wished to be baptized in the name of the Lord to come forward and kneel before him. Even after the decision I had made the night before, I wondered if I still had a choice. What would happen if I didn't follow the others? Guilt burned in my mind as I fell into place in the middle of the line.

In a moment, I was kneeling on that rough, dirty, and cracked cement floor in my black dress, and it was my turn to repeat the vows that I would stay in the Amish church for the rest of my life. People stood around us, wearing black clothes and solemn faces.

As I repeated the words Bishop Dan spoke, I tried to blink back the tears. Then Bishop Dan cupped his hands over my head and the deacon poured water into them. Bishop Dan said, "I baptize you in the name of the Father, the Son, and the Holy Ghost, Amen," and poured the water from his hands onto my head. My tears were one with the holy water that dripped down over my face.

Bishop Dan gave the "holy kiss" to his son and had a woman come forward to give it to the girls, as was customary. Henry Kate, who had been holding my head covering for me, replaced it on my head; then she helped me off my knees and kissed me on the cheek, my formal acceptance into the church. It felt so out of place. Except for *shmunzling* by the young men I had dated, I had never been hugged or kissed by anyone in the community.

When all five of us had been baptized and welcomed into the church with a holy kiss, Bishop Dan asked us to take our seats. The dark and solemn occasion made me feel more trapped than ever, not the new person I had hoped I'd become. I could not stop the tears from streaming down my face.

When we got home, Sarah said to me, "Lomie, why were you crying at your baptism?"

It was just like Sarah to have noticed. Sometimes it felt as though she could see inside me and know what I was thinking or feeling.

"A lot of people cry at their baptisms," I said.

"Were they happy tears?"

"Of course."

"They didn't look happy."

I got up and left the room.

TWO WEEKS AFTER MY baptism, I had to sit through my first Council meeting, the extra long church service that takes place twice a year, in which the bishop reviews the *Ordnung*. The regular church services were three hours long. Council meeting was even longer and lasted until after the midday meal. A small group of women left to go eat at a table set up in a different part of the house, and a group of men ate at the men's table. When all the church members had eaten in shifts and were sitting in their seats on the backless benches, the bishop began talking about the *Ordnung*. First he went through what was not allowed for farm machinery and other modern conveniences. Then he started talking about the way men should dress: wear suspenders, no zippers or snaps on their pants; black shoes, unless they were for work, and then wear shoes as plain as possible; wear their hair so it would cover half their ears; and wear their beards untrimmed.

Bishop Dan shuffled his feet and said in a bored voice, "Aah-and, the women should wear their dresses in the right pattern and the proper length, and when they leave home wear the appropriate cape and apron, as well as bonnets in the summer and shawls in winter. They need to wear black shoes and socks, and cutting their hair isn't allowed. They need to wear their hair according to the *Ordnung*, and their *koppa* should cover most of their hair. They should wear pins in their dresses instead of buttons, and they are responsible for dressing their children according to the *Ordnung* as well."

Bishop Dan shuffled his feet again and he said, "Now, if there is anything that I missed, it doesn't mean it is allowed. Just because I haven't mentioned it doesn't excuse people from not obeying the *Ordnung*."

I went home from church feeling completely emptied out. I was more fatigued than I would have been if I had been cleaning house all day. I wasn't used to sitting for a whole day, being told what I was not permitted to do. I wasn't looking forward to another long service, which would be our communion service, just two weeks away. I would have to sit for another whole day on the uncomfortable backless benches.

TWO WEEKS LATER, at the communion service—several hours after the children and young people who had not yet joined church had been dismissed, and just when I thought I could not sit a moment longer—the deacon brought in a jug and round loaves of bread. He placed them on a table.

Then Bishop Dan asked us all to rise. He talked about the bread in a solemn tone: "First, in the spring, the ground is prepared. Then the seed is sown. The weeds are plucked from the fields as the wheat grows. When the grain ripens, it is cut. When the right time comes, the wheat is harvested and the grain separated from the straw and ground into meal. Then it goes through the wives' hands and is kneaded into bread. As the grains joined to make this bread, they gave up their individuality. In the same way that each grain gave up its individuality to become part of the bread, so must we give up our individuality to become a part of the community."

After that, I couldn't concentrate on what Bishop Dan was saying. I was thinking about the concept of giving up one's individuality to be a part of the community. Was I willing, or even able to do that? I thought to myself, at least the grains had been fully developed "individuals" to start with. Didn't we need to be individuals first, before we *could* come together as a community?

I imagined the grains being ground on a grindstone. I wanted to be one of the grains that would fall by the wayside, to escape being ground.

I wondered if I was the only one in the whole congregation who had these feelings and thoughts. I chided myself for having wayward thoughts at my first communion, and forced myself to concentrate on the service.

Bishop Dan continued: "Jesus said, 'This is my body, when you eat of it, remember me.'" I watched the bishop, two ministers, and the deacon exchange communion bread. Then the deacon followed Bishop Dan with thick slices of bread as they walked up to the oldest man in the congregation, Al Miller. Dan broke off a small piece and handed it to him. Al ate the bread, bowed, and then sat down. The bishop moved down the line, giving the men communion bread. They all put the bread in their mouths, bowed, and sat down. Noah, the bishop's son, was the last man to receive communion bread. Then Dan and the deacon walked to Al Miller's wife, Ada, and served her bread. He started with the older women and worked his way down to us young women. I was the third to the last to eat my communion bread. I bowed and sat down.

When they were done with the bread, they had us all rise again to receive the wine. Bishop Dan went on to describe the process grapes go through to become wine, focusing again on how the individual grapes give up their identity to make the wine.

Then he and the deacon passed the cup around. As I saw Datt drink from the cup, I realized I had to drink from the same one. Purple drips trickled down the side of the white enamel. The bishop had told everyone how we should not shy away from drinking from the cup just because others had drunk from it. I wanted to say, *That is easy for you to say; you got the first drink*. I was never more aware of how the community sorted people first by gender, then by age. Even the youngest male got his drink of wine before the eldest woman in the church. My place in the church was always behind Sara Mae Gingerich, who was one day older than me.

When it was my turn to drink from the cup, I remembered how Datt had already drunk from it. I turned it around and drank from just above the handle.

After communion came the foot washing. The deacon carried in four buckets of warm water and towels. Chairs were set up in the front, and the older men started to wash one another's feet, using two sets of chairs, while two older women did the same. I was happy to see that the men and women had separate buckets of water. After each pair had washed one another's feet, they shook hands and gave one another the holy kiss. Bishop Dan said we shouldn't think about whose feet we washed, because we were all the same in the eyes of the Lord. When it was Elizabeth Gingerich's and my turn to wash one another's feet, we took off our shoes and socks. Then she splashed the warm water over my feet and dried them off with the damp towel that half the women before us had used. Then I washed her feet, and we exchanged the holy kiss. We put our shoes and socks back on. My feet were still damp, and my socks stuck to my skin in an uncomfortable way. I reminded myself that it didn't matter—it was the humility of the ritual that counted.

As we passed through the doorway, the deacon sat there, holding a navy-blue cloth bag. We all put money in the bag, our contribution to the church fund that would help out families in need, especially those with big hospital bills. In the washhouse, we gathered our shawls and bonnets and prepared for the walk home. Communion service was considered a serious time and we were all expected to be more solemn than usual, so even afterwards we remained subdued.

At home, I lay on my bed and stared at the ceiling. Now that I had had my first communion, I would never be able to leave the Amish. If there was one thing worse than leaving the Amish before baptism, it was leaving after baptism. Somewhere in the High German phrases I had repeated after the bishop, I had promised to stay with the Amish church my whole life long. This was the time I was supposed to be sure that joining church was the right thing for me, and I was more uncertain than I'd ever been.

I was hungry. I went downstairs and ate popcorn, then two pieces of apple pie, followed by a piece of cake. I felt bloated. I walked out to the woods and threw up, then covered it with leaves.

What Do You Mean by Love?

Sarah started going to singings soon after I did. She was shy, and hung back until I taught her how to dance. With her tall figure and bright blue eyes, she drew stares from the young men. The first few times she attended the singings, she rode home with me and whoever asked me for a date, or in the taxi we called if no one asked me for one. One night, Sarah and I were dancing together when a young man cut me out to dance with her. Later that night, he asked her for a date, and she said yes.

His name was Sonny Miller, and he was romantic and talkative. To my amazement, I found myself riding home on a buggy with my younger sister and her date. At nineteen, I suddenly felt ancient.

When Susan joined the young people, she immediately began dating one boy after another. I wondered how she was so popular when she was one of "Sim's girls," too. I got a few rides with her and her dates before she got tired of me. She criticized me for talking too much. Before a month was out, she was going steady with a boy named Robert, and then almost immediately, Sarah and Sonny started going steady as well. I felt not only ancient, but well on my way to becoming a spinster.

One night at a singing, I was asked for a date with Milo's Mel's Dan, who is a cousin to Sonny. I found him fun to talk to on the way home. It seemed good to have my own ride again.

When we reached my home, we went through the usual rituals of going to bed, clothed. As soon as we started to *shmunzle*, I decided the ride had not been worth it. His kisses made me want to turn my back and go to sleep. At least, I thought as the endless night dragged on, he didn't push his luck to see how far he could go.

WHEN DAN ASKED ME for another date a week later, I was astounded. No one had asked me for a second date for so long that I caught myself saying yes just because I was so flattered. Besides, I really needed a ride home. And that night, his kisses didn't seem so bad. He seemed to like to listen to me talk in the buggy, and before I knew it, he'd driven me home nine times in a row.

Was this love, I wondered? It felt more like a habit. Not at all what I'd expected.

The following week when I was working at one of the six houses I cleaned, I got a call. It was a man, and he was panting. His voice was nearly inaudible. I could barely make out the words: "Hi this is Dan—I was just wondering if it would be all right to go steady."

Stunned, I pressed the receiver to my ear, listening to his loud breathing. Could I say yes? I could already feel the weight of many burdens slipping away from me. Would it be so bad? My own home, my own babies. But with Dan? Night after night, wishing he were someone else? For the rest of my life?

Dan interrupted my thoughts when he spoke. "You don't have to answer me right now—you can tell me later."

Deep in my heart, I knew what my answer would be. "Okay," I said, and I was ready to add, "I already know what my answer is."

But Dan had hung up.

When I came home from work that day, Sarah was in the basement kitchen cooking a new concoction with tomatoes and zucchini. The aroma of the spices she was using was tantalizing even to my taste buds, and I didn't like tomatoes.

Sarah turned around when I came down the stairs and said, "Lomieeee," with a big smile on her face.

"What?" I asked, with a straight face. I thought, *Darn! She knows!*

"You know . . . Come on . . . I already know about it."

"About what?"

"Didn't Dan call you at work today?"

"What if he did, why do you care? And how would you know?"

"Sonny called me at work today and told me. Well? You are going to say yes, aren't you?"

I could have said I didn't want to tell her, or that I had to think about it longer. But, instead I said, "No."

"Why not?"

"Because I don't love him."

She looked reproachfully at me. "Lomie! You've had nine dates with him. Why did you lead him on if you don't feel anything for him?"

I felt a cramp knot my stomach. *Because I hated to ride home with you and Sonny? Because I'll do anything to get away from Datt?* "I—I was trying to find out if I loved him or not," I said lamely.

"What do you mean by love?" Sarah asked.

"Love is what you and Sonny have. I can see it in your faces."

Sarah said, "What Sonny and I have is unusual. It's different for everyone, you know. Would you even recognize love? Maybe you need to think about how you feel about Susan and me both going steady when you aren't." Sarah's voice followed me up the stairs. "You may not get another chance like this for a long time."

"It is my decision, not yours!" I shouted down.

"I just hope you make the right one," Sarah called.

Her words echoed in my mind all the way to my room.

I made the wrong choice. That Sunday when Dan drove me home, I said yes when I meant no. I was glad the dark hid the lie in my face.

WHEN I CLEANED THE BIG houses in Chesterland, I sometimes watched soap operas on television in the afternoons. I thought the troubles in the soap operas were glamorous compared to my own life.

One day I found a *Yankee* magazine at work. I looked at all the pictures of New England. I had liked pictures of New England ever since I saw them in my seventh-grade geography book. Ohio had woods and fields like New England's, but I'd never seen mountains before. I liked the mountains of New England that cradled farms and towns in their foothills.

My favorite of all the states was Vermont, so I read every article I could find about it. In this copy of *Yankee* magazine, I saw an ad for a magazine called

Vermont Life. I thought about sending for it, but I hesitated, knowing I would
have to use my allowance money. But a week later when I was in the same
house, I found the address again and sent for the magazine.

Two weeks later, the first one arrived. We rarely got magazines—mostly
just the *Farmer's Almanac.* As usual, Datt didn't seem to notice what I had done.
Mem seemed surprised when she saw the magazine. "Why are you spending
your money on frivolous things like that?" she asked. But later, I found her
with the magazine open.

Alone in my room, I gazed at all the pictures and read the magazine from
cover to cover. My favorite picture was taken in North Pomfret. It showed an
old Cape-style house with a birch tree on one side and a maple on the other.
The branches were bare under a deep blue sky, with the last of the leaves
scattered on the green grass. Off in the distance, cotton-white clouds hung
above the hilly landscape. Near the horizon, mountains touched the fluffy
clouds. It reminded me of the psalm from the Bible: *I will lift mine eyes unto
the hills, from whence cometh my help.*

When I turned the page, I saw a picture of a stream running underneath
a covered bridge, with a woman sitting on a stone wall nearby. Beyond the
covered bridge was an old white house with dark red shutters. The caption
read, "What is the young lady thinking as she watches the Green River pass
underneath a covered bridge south of Guilford Center?"

I knew what I would be thinking: that I had made it to the land of my
dreams, many miles away from my troubles. I would not leave the spot on the
stone wall until I was sure I wouldn't wake and find I was dreaming.

Now that three of his daughters were going steady with boys and Lizzie
was almost twenty-one, Datt began to lecture us girls every evening about
the importance of obedience, followed up with German quotes from the
Bible that none of us understood—and then his monologue would become
jumbled and cease to make any sense at all. But we didn't dare walk away, lest
we trigger his violence.

When Lizzie was twenty-one years old, considered "of age" in the
community, she surprised us all and moved in with Amanda, whom she had
befriended at the few singings Joe had taken her to. Amanda's parents were
willing to take Lizzie in as long as she paid room and board. Not long after

she moved in with Amanda's family, Lizzie found out that Amanda's father and our mother had dated when they were young. She felt that she had found her "rightful" sister, or the sister she would have had if Mem and Amanda's father had gotten married. Lizzie had fancied herself adopted ever since she was old enough to understand the concept. It was her way of accounting for always feeling like an outsider within the family.

I felt guilty that I had not been a better sister to Lizzie; at the same time, I envied her new freedom.

Datt now focused on the rest of us. Susan and I most often bore the brunt of his rage, because Sarah had a sneaky way of not getting caught, even though she did many of the same things we did. He thought Sarah was the only obedient daughter he had. He held a grudge against Susan for calling the police when he had hurt Lizzie's leg several years before. I had been at work that day. When I came home, Lizzie had a swollen leg that she couldn't walk on, and Datt had a bright red burn mark on his arm.

Lizzie had been ironing when Datt came after her because she refused to sit down to eat at the table. She held up the iron and said, "Datt, if you come near me, I will burn you with this iron!" He kept coming at her and she burned his arm. That still didn't stop Datt. He kept hitting her.

Mem kept yelling, "Sim, *shtopp sell! Sim, shtopp sell!*" He wouldn't stop. Susan ran next door and called the police.

Lizzie dropped the iron and ran for the door to get away from Datt. He caught her leg in the door and slammed the door on her leg over and over, nearly breaking it. By the time the policeman came, the struggle was over. Datt was sitting in his rocking chair, and Lizzie had dragged herself backwards up the stairway, to her room. Her leg was bruised from below her knee all the way to her hip.

The policeman came upstairs and looked at Lizzie's bruised leg. He asked her if she wanted to go to the hospital. She said no. He asked her if she wanted to press charges and she said no.

Lizzie told me later that she and Datt made a confession in a church service that was held at our house. Bishop Dan had Datt make his confession first, and then Lizzie was brought in to kneel down and make her confession. She said she could only focus on the pain in her leg, which was nearly unbearable.

Perhaps it was because Susan had called the police, or because she wore the "slickest" clothing, with shorter dresses and smaller *koppa*, but it seemed like Datt was after Susan more than anyone.

One day, when I came home from work, I found Susan and Sarah standing by the cedar chest in their room. Susan was sobbing.

"I was ironing," she told me, "and Datt asked me out of nowhere why I comb my hair the way I do." She drew a shuddering breath. "I didn't know what to say that wouldn't trigger him to go crazy, so I didn't say anything. He kept shouting, 'Answer me! Answer me!' Finally I said, 'I don't know.'"

"'Well, why don't you know?' Datt yelled at me. And when I didn't answer, he jumped up out of his rocking chair and started hitting me all over, the way he does when he goes crazy."

Sarah and I didn't say anything. We knew.

"I refused to let him know it hurt, so I braced myself and let him hit me. By the time Mem got there, I was starting to faint. The last thing I remember was hearing her shouting, 'Sim, you have to stop! You are going to kill her!'"

Tears choked her voice. Susan put her hands over her face. I cried too, feeling helpless and trapped by Datt's violence. When he came after someone, there was no fighting back—he was physically strong, but when he was in one of his rages, he was as strong as a bull, and just as wild.

"We have to do something," I said through my own tears.

"But what?" Sarah asked. As the three of us stood there, crying around the cedar chest at the foot end of Sarah's bed, I thought how much the chest was like a coffin. It was as if our hope had died in the chest. Our fear of Datt's violence kept us trapped so that we could not even imagine freedom.

ON THE NEXT CHURCH SUNDAY, at a service in the Shrocks' living room, Bishop Dan asked all the church members to stay seated. This was a common practice at the end of church services, when there were issues to be discussed by the church members only. I had always been curious about what actually happened behind those closed doors. Now that I was a member of the church, I would find out.

The realization of what was happening crept up on me slowly. First I noticed Datt leave with the children and young folks who hadn't yet joined church, and I thought maybe he was going to the barn for a break.

When all was quiet, Bishop Dan began talking about "the brother" who had come to him and wanted to make things right. Then he said, "He wants to confess that he lost his temper the other day and hit one of the daughters." Bishop Dan paused, then continued, "Sim was talking to her and she wasn't listening, so he told her to answer him. She tried running from him, and therefore he hit her. Now he wants to make his confession, since he feels he went a bit too far."

I could feel my face getting red with shame when I realized this "brother" was Datt. Then the bishop added his own commentary: "But it's not entirely Sim's fault. If the wife and children would be more obedient, then Sim wouldn't have this problem. Since that is the case, I will take his confession sitting down, instead of having him get on his knees, if no one has any objection to that." With that, Bishop Dan sent the deacon around to ask everyone's approval for this decision.

I thought I would die of shame and indignation. Bishop Dan was giving us a vote about whether Datt should confess sitting or kneeling! If someone disagrees, will he have Datt kneel for his confession after all? What if someone disagrees with the whole charade?

The torture of sitting there on the backless bench with the deacon shuffling closer and closer to me, getting one submissive yes after another from the girls before me, was almost more than I could bear. Then he stood in front of me and it was my turn to say yes. I knew that women in the church were not allowed to oppose anything. They had to tell their husbands if they disagreed with the policies of the church, and then it was the men's duty to relay that information to the bishop. According to this policy, I had no choice. But to say yes was a lie. I was fighting back the tears that wanted to spill out of my eyes and down my cheeks, and I tried to find my voice. No sound came out, even though my mouth had made the motion.

The deacon leaned closer and said, "What?"

I had to live through the agony twice. I wanted to shout, *No! I don't agree with any part of this because that is not how it happened! She didn't try to run away at all because he was hitting her so hard, she couldn't! He didn't even tell you that "the daughter" fainted from him hitting her! Now do you hear me?*

Instead, I swallowed hard and tried again. This time I managed to muster something close to a yes, and the deacon shuffled on to the next person.

When Datt was brought in, he had his hat in his hands, and he bent his head so far down, I wondered how he could walk. I imagined this was his posture the day he arrived to see Mem when she was living at her aunt Em's house before they were married. This dejected form had convinced Mem to marry Datt, even against her *besser gewisser* (better knowing).

Bishop Dan had Datt sit on the bench in front of him and repeat something in German I didn't understand. Datt said it in a voice so meek and childlike, I thought that if I didn't know him I would wonder how he could be violent at all. Then the bishop pardoned him and Datt took his original seat.

I held in all my feelings until later that day, when I asked Mem if a woman had ever opposed anything in the church. She said, "Not that I know of."

"How is a woman supposed to talk to her husband when she isn't even sitting with him, anyway?" I asked. "By the time she has a chance to say something to him after the church service, the decisions are already made."

"I've often wondered that myself," Mem said in a musing voice. Then she seemed to catch herself and she added, "Oh Lomie, if you only knew how much better off you are without asking these questions, maybe you wouldn't ask them."

I asked, "So what is my way of communicating to the bishop if I disagree? I don't have a husband."

Mem sighed. "It's supposedly through Datt."

I just looked at her for a long moment, then said, "So, I had to lie? Because I had to do it, it's not considered a lie, is that it?" My voice rose with the panic I felt at the injustice of it all.

"Oh Lomie, you are just making it harder on yourself," Mem said.

I went to my room and lay down. I couldn't even talk to Sarah and Susan about what had happened, because they weren't church members yet, so it was forbidden. Exhausted, I fell asleep.

I dreamed that I was in the picture in my *Vermont Life* magazine. I was under the maple tree's bare limbs, with the fallen leaves still fresh on the grass. I stood there and looked into the house, knowing I would go in, but first I wanted to run down the big hill toward the mountains on the horizon. As I started running, I discovered I could run like I had in my childhood dreams. I floated just above the green, green grass and landed lightly, then pushed off and floated down the hill to my next landing place. I thought, "I have dreamed this so many times, but this time it's real! I am as free as a butterfly!" I sailed along toward the mountains, feeling the breeze through my hair streaming out behind me.

When I first heard my name, it was part of the dream, and I turned to see who was calling me. Then I couldn't see the maple tree and the house anymore, and I wondered if I had gotten lost.

"Lomie!" This time the voice was insistent and impatient, accompanied by knocking at the door. I knew I was waking from a dream, and I wanted so much to stay in the dream instead of on my bed in Mem and Datt's house. Then someone shook me, and I looked up into Sarah's face. She said, "Dan is here."

I had to drag myself away from the dream to comb my hair, put on my *kopp*, and smooth out the wrinkles in my dress before Dan came up to my room. More than ever, I realized how Dan didn't belong in my future if I ever dared to follow my dreams.

Wrapping a Plan

avid pulled into a gas station in Massachusetts. The trip was getting long, and I felt sorry that he and Tim still had to drive after they dropped me off. They would not arrive home until after midnight. After refueling the car, we decided to eat a quick meal. I asked David if he wanted me to drive, and he said it would be a good idea, given that he had three hours to go with Tim after he dropped me off.

Back on the road, Tim became restless and asked why he had had to come along. I asked him whether he was sorry he did, and he said, no, he was glad he had come. He bounced around in the back seat before finally finding a comfortable position for the remainder of the trip.

When we finally pulled up to Green Street, and David helped me bring my luggage to my room on the third floor, I kissed him good-bye and asked him to call me when they arrived home, even if it woke me up.

I found a potted plant outside my door, with a card signed from the women in the house. I felt touched by their sympathy. I had only known them for a month, but they were already my friends.

As I lay on my bed, inside the window that looked out over the roof of the science building, I had a harder time relaxing and falling asleep than I had expected. My thoughts went back in time again, to the few months when I was going steady with my Amish boyfriend.

DAN AND I SAW EACH OTHER every week. He would come in the afternoon on Sunday and leave at four in the morning, so he could drive home before the sun came up, which was the tradition.

We sometimes visited Dan's close friend, Eddie, who had curly black hair. He was short and slight. He had several dozen arrowheads that he had found on his father's farm over the years, which fascinated me. I asked him how he found them. Eddie said he walked along the furrows after the fields had been freshly plowed. Dan said, "Yes, but anyone else can be walking along the same path and not see them." Eddie blushed, and I could tell he was embarrassed by the compliment.

I sometimes wished I could quit going with Dan and have dates with Eddie. But I knew there was no guarantee Eddie would ask me, even if I did quit Dan. Besides, my fantasies included going out to dinner together and getting to know one another through conversations, so *shmunzling* would have more meaning. Still, even just thinking about *shmunzling* with Eddie was more sensual than all the nights I had spent with Dan.

I tried having romantic feelings for Dan. When Sarah and Sonny went for walks with a blanket and found a comfortable spot under a tree away from the house for privacy, I initiated those kinds of encounters with Dan. In early October, I took him for a walk in what my sisters and I called the autumn woods. My favorite spot was next to a giant oak with a natural spring nearby. The maple trees shed bright red and gold leaves, creating a colorful carpet on the ground. Dan and I sat there next to one another. I wanted to just be there and not say or do anything, but I couldn't get away from Dan's face always in mine, his persistent but empty kisses always in the way. I finally got up and walked towards home. After that, the spot with the spring wasn't special to me anymore.

Once Dan came on Saturday night instead of Sunday. Datt said nothing when he went upstairs, but I saw the dark look, and knew I would be in trouble in the morning for having a boy spend the night on a Saturday. In other families it was okay for young people to occasionally date on Saturday nights. But whenever Mem and Datt had the chance to be stricter and more old-fashioned than anyone in the community, they took it.

Dan and I hadn't explored below each other's necks. After we'd been kissing for a while, I was bored, so I guided his hands to my breasts. Then something happened that I was not ready for. He started breathing hard, so that it felt as though his heavy breathing was using up the air around me. I slid out of the bed quickly, saying I needed to use the outhouse. I hoped he would calm down while I was gone.

When I came out of the outhouse, I saw someone moving in the darkness. For a second I thought it was Dan, but then I heard Datt shouting, telling me how I was a member of the church, how I wasn't supposed to have a boy over on Saturday nights, and how I should be ashamed of my behavior. I ran for my room. I knew Datt could barge up behind me, though I had never heard of any Amish parents doing that before. It just wasn't done. But when Datt was in one of his moods, I couldn't count on any taboo holding him back from his craziness.

"What's the matter?" Dan asked when I came back in. I could see him in the moonlight, sitting up in bed, looking like a scrawny teenager. For the first time, I was glad of his presence.

"Datt doesn't want you here on a Saturday night," I said, trying to get my breath back.

He got up and put his shirt on. "Let's go to my house," he said. I knew Datt would be twice as mad at me when I got back home. On the other hand, he might have forgotten about the whole thing, so running seemed like a reasonable choice.

Dan went to hitch up his horse. In a few moments, he brought him to the front door, and I slipped down in my white nightdress, climbed into the buggy, and we took off. We saw no sign of Datt.

It was a ten-mile ride to Dan's house. I used the opportunity to fill Dan in on Datt's pattern of outbursts. He listened, but didn't say anything, or offer me any of the comfort and understanding that I so craved. I thought that if he could only be sympathetic, I might be wrong about him.

It was clear that he didn't want to get involved.

Maybe Dan will want to break up with me after tonight, I thought, riding along beside him through the cool, star-filled night. A tendril of anger crept into my thoughts, bringing hard knowledge with it.

If joining church had not made things any better for me, then probably marrying Dan wouldn't either.

We spent the rest of the night in Dan's bed, doing the same boring things we always did. I had learned my lesson about exploring any new territory. I put up with the empty kisses. I was glad he didn't push me.

Nothing was said the next day when I returned home.

A FEW NIGHTS LATER, I had been asleep for less than an hour when Mem shook my shoulder, saying, "You girls need to wake up."

"What is going on?" Sarah asked, sleepily. I buried my head under my pillow, prepared to sleep through it, whatever it was.

Mem sounded worried. "Susan took off and she hasn't come back. You have to go find her."

"She'll come back," I said from under my pillow. The previous summer, she had hidden in the back of a trailer the next-door neighbors were moving to Texas, but she had started screaming when the trailer was closed up, because she felt like she had no air.

"I don't think she has any clothes on," Mem said in a very low voice.

"What?" I asked, coming out from under the pillow.

"She was taking a shower in the basement when Datt went after her."

Sarah got up and pulled on her dress. I got up, too.

"Where is he now?" I asked.

"In bed," Mem said. "I think you should go to the Gingeriches and check if she went there. It's too cold for her to stay in the woods. I will stay here, in case she comes back."

Sarah grabbed Susan's bathrobe, and then we started by looking in the sugarhouse, then beyond in the dark woods, calling her all the way. Then we went in the other direction, working our way to the Gingeriches' house. They said they hadn't seen Susan.

"This is so embarrassing," Sarah said as we started back home. "It's bad enough that neighbors always know what happens in our family without us having to tell them."

I agreed. I was tempted to describe for Sarah what it was like to have to sit through one of Datt's confessions in church, but I decided I had better not.

We kept calling as we walked down Hale Road, next to the woods. Finally, on the hill above our house, we thought we heard something. We called again, and this time there was a distinct answer. We followed the sound of Susan's voice to the Hale's sugarhouse.

"I'm in here," she said. We opened the door, and there was Susan, lying on the floor, wrapped in a towel with a half-slip on. Sarah gave Susan the bathrobe, and then we gave her our coats, one to wear, one to wrap around her waist. "Let's go home," I said.

"But where is Datt?" Susan asked. She was shivering so hard from fear and cold that she could hardly talk.

"He is in bed," I said.

"Are you sure? How do you know he isn't waiting outside for me to come back?"

"No, Mem said he is in bed," we assured her.

After we started back down the lane, I asked, "What happened?"

Susan said through her shivering, "I was taking a shower downstairs when I heard Datt get up from his rocking chair and run out of the living room, like he was coming after me. Maybe it was the scraping noise of the wash basin against the cement that triggered him, I don't know. You know the sound of Datt's stomping feet when he's angry. I grabbed this towel and my half-slip and ran out the north door of the basement." She sobbed and shivered. "What are we going to do? We can't keep wondering what is coming next."

Susan's question was on my mind when I went to Megan's house in Chesterland the next day. Megan was a young Catholic mother of four little ones, and I had been cleaning and watching the children for her once a week for the past few months. I paid a man named Mr. Pell to give me a ride there every Wednesday. I didn't like sitting in the front seat with him, because he chewed gum noisily.

That day, Megan left me with the children and a large batch of ironing. I wasn't in any shape to do either. I spent most of my time out of sight of the children, in the bathroom, crying. I knew one thing for sure. I couldn't endure the violence and the fear any longer. I had no idea what I was going to do, but something had to change.

I was still crying in the bathroom when Megan came home, earlier than I had expected. I quickly washed my face and slipped down to the basement to iron.

Megan noticed that I had just begun the work. After one look at my face, though, she didn't reprimand me.

"Saloma, what is the matter?" she asked.

No one had ever asked me that question before. I collapsed into the nearest chair. Dimly aware of the children's inquisitive stares, I covered my face with my hands. I couldn't hold back the sobs and I couldn't talk. Megan herded her children up the stairs and into the playroom. Then she came down and said, "You need to tell me what this is about."

I had my crying under control by then and I said, "It has nothing to do with you. It's got to do with home. My father hurts us girls because he thinks we are rebellious. But there is no way we can please him, because he is unreasonable. Last night my sister was taking a bath in the basement, and she heard my father coming after her. She escaped into the woods. She stayed out there with hardly any clothes until Sarah and I found her."

Megan looked at me with a stunned expression. She said, "Saloma, I had no idea."

"You didn't?" I asked. I thought everyone in the world knew about my family.

"Does he ever hit your mother?" Megan asked.

"No, just us. He seems to hate when we show signs of growing up. If we all stayed children, I think he would be fine."

"You can't go on living like this," Megan said.

"My sisters and I say that to each other so many times, but we never know what to do about it."

"There is a place here in Chesterland called Head Help. I will go upstairs and call them and make an appointment for you to see them next week when you come here. Will you be all right until then?"

I laughed at the irony. "I've lived with it so far, I think I can go another week," I said.

I ironed while Megan made the phone call. She came downstairs and told me she had arranged for me to see a woman named Carol the following week.

CAROL WORE SO MANY bracelets and necklaces, she rattled when she moved. She had a headful of dark, curly hair. She asked me to describe for her what was happening in my family. I did.

"How old are you?" Carol asked.

"Twenty."

"When do you turn twenty-one?"

"Next June. Why?"

"In the state of Ohio, it is not legal for us to intervene in a family situation when the report comes from someone under twenty-one. Do you have an older brother or sister who would give us that permission?"

My hopes were dashed immediately. I felt as though I were watching them sink in deep water, like a stone.

"No. I have an older brother who is married. He wouldn't want to get involved. He might tell my parents I reported this, and it would make the situation worse," I said.

"Is there anybody else?"

"I have an older sister, but she isn't living at home right now. I would also be concerned about her telling my parents."

"Then we need to ask your mother's permission. What is your parents' phone number?"

"We don't have a phone."

"Then this will take longer, because whoever makes contact with your mother has to write to her and wait for her response. I am not the person to help you. I am going to need to assign a social worker to your family. Her name is June. She needs to get permission from a family member who's at least twenty-one."

I told Carol how important it was to not let Mem know who had alerted them. I shivered when I imagined the consequences of that. Then I gave Carol the phone numbers and a schedule where I cleaned houses, so June could call me and let me know what Mem's response was.

I didn't think that Mem would say yes to the help, but there was at least a glimmer of hope. Sometimes she talked to us girls about how she didn't know what to do about Datt's violent outbursts. We would appeal to her to get outside help, but Mem would sigh her deep sigh and say she didn't know who to go to.

Then, the next day, or a few hours later, Mem would take everything back by saying, "Oh, if you girls could just be less rebellious, then maybe Datt wouldn't have these problems." We would point out the times when he was triggered by nothing we said or did, as if his violence had a life of its own. But Mem would purse her lips and not say anything, leaving us with only each other for allies.

A dim hope was better than no hope at all, and so I hoped Mem would accept the help offered to her.

WHEN I GOT HOME that afternoon, I asked Sarah and Susan to come upstairs. When we were gathered around the cedar chest once again, I told them what I'd done. To my surprise, they started questioning me.

"What if Mem finds out it was you?" Susan asked.

"You absolutely cannot tell her," I said.

"What if it doesn't work?" Sarah asked.

"Then we are in the same boat we are in now. Nothing has worked so far, has it?"

They grudgingly agreed. They also agreed not to tell Mem that it was me who had alerted the social workers.

When Mem got the letter several days later, she would not let us see it, and she wouldn't tell us anything about the contents, except that someone had "reported" us.

I didn't lie. I only said to her, "Is it really important that we know who reported it? Isn't it more important that we use this chance to help Datt and therefore help the whole family?"

Mem's shoulders slumped lower over the potatoes she was peeling. She shook her head and said with a Mem sigh, "Oh, I just don't know." I thought she was close to saying yes, so I left it at that.

Four days later, June called me at Megan's house and said, "I have just gotten a letter from your mother. Did she tell you what her answer was?"

"No, I didn't even know she had sent you an answer," I said.

"She hasn't said yes. She said she wanted to work through the church," June said.

I didn't know my reaction was audible until June asked me what the matter was.

"I know what she means by that, and it hasn't worked yet. It may be making it worse."

"Do you want to tell me about it?"

"I am not allowed to talk about anything that happens in church."

June paused and said, "It sounds like your mother was close to saying yes. I can send her another letter and try again, if you would like me to."

"All right," I said, but the light of my hope had dimmed so much it might as well have gone out.

"I will do that; then I will call you and let you know. Are there any changes in these phone numbers that you gave me?"

"No, they are all the same."

Two weeks later, I was at the Snyders' house. The Snyders had lost their fifteen-year-old daughter in a car accident less than a year before. I cleaned her room every two weeks when I cleaned the rest of their spacious home. The room had been kept exactly as it was when Pamela was alive. I was cleaning Pamela's room when the phone rang. Mrs. Snyder came to the door and said it was for me. I picked up the black receiver from the white dresser and said, "Hello," as I listened to my heartbeat in my ears.

It was June. She said, "I've gotten another letter from your mother. She has said no again."

I was quiet until I trusted my voice. I was glad she couldn't see the tears that were already spilling down my cheeks. I asked, "What else can we do?"

"There isn't anything else I can do. When do you turn twenty-one?"

"Next June," I said.

"If there isn't any change by then, you can give us another call," June said.

I wanted to say, *But nine months is the same as never! Even one more month is unbearable, let alone nine!*

June said she was very sorry. Her voice sounded far away as she said, "If you ever need someone to talk to, give me a call."

I wanted to shout, *What good is it to talk about things, if we can't do anything about it!* Instead I said a meek "Thank you," then hung up as quickly as I could. I knew I couldn't hold back my tears much longer.

I put the black receiver back on the phone and lay down on Pamela's bed. I realized Mrs. Snyder could walk in and find me there, but I had to take that risk because at that moment I could not stand on my own feet. As I lay there, I wished I was dead instead of Pamela. I didn't understand why God would take away the Snyders' daughter when they loved her so much, and yet I had to live this unbearable life in a family in which I did not feel loved.

Before Mem had said no to June, I hadn't allowed myself to think about any other options to get out of this situation. Now I was forced to. I could think of only two—suicide, and leaving the Amish. First I considered suicide. I wondered if that could be any worse than my unbearable life. I considered how I might manage it. Maybe I could run out in front of a speeding car. But what if I only managed to get maimed and I didn't die? I knew I didn't have the guts to go through with suicide. It was probably just as well, I decided, because I knew I would go straight to Hell if I did. But according to Amish beliefs, I would go to Hell if I left the Amish, too. Then a daring thought came to me. If I was going to Hell for leaving the Amish, I would at least have a lifetime on earth before I had to go to Hell. And besides, I thought, *What if the preachers are wrong?* A feeling of adventure and excitement came with my thoughts of a whole new life, away from my family and all its troubles. Before I got up from Pamela's bed, I resolved one thing in my mind—I could no longer think of what was good for the family. I now had to think of what was good for me.

A FEW DAYS LATER, I was on my way to the mailbox when I walked by Datt as he was sawing a piece of wood in half between two sawhorses. Mem had asked him to get some firewood to take the chill off the living room, where she was going to set up the oval galvanized tub for taking baths. Datt was sawing some logs in half that were too long from the previous winter's supply of wood. He didn't look up.

"Lomie, take these into the house," he said.

"No, I'm getting the mail right now," I said in an impatient and angry tone.

Datt looked up at me, his blank eyes startled. I knew my mistake was made. I had never dared say no to Datt before, and neither had I dared show any anger toward him.

Datt was too shocked to respond at that moment. I ran into the house, down the stairs, through the basement, and out the north entrance, heading for the cornfield behind the barn. I plowed through the cornfield into the woods beyond before looking back to see if Datt was pursuing me. He wasn't. As soon as I'd reached the thick trees, I found a place to hide and sat down on a stump.

There was no sound of pursuit for a long time. Then, later, I heard Mem calling me. I didn't answer, knowing full well I was making things worse for myself. But I knew one thing for sure: I needed time to think. I had never talked to Datt that way, and I wasn't about to find out what my punishment was going to be.

Mem stopped calling me. I stayed in the woods, thinking about making an escape. I thought about walking out to Forest Road and up to Route 322 and hitchhiking to anywhere from there. But what if a man who wasn't to be trusted picked me up?

When the sun was low on the horizon, I wanted to get up and start walking in the direction of escape while I still had light, but my legs wouldn't let me. I was getting cold. I wished I had grabbed my coat on the way out of the house. But then again, I might not have gotten out of there before Datt would have hurt me.

With no coat, only the clothes on my back, and no money, I didn't think I was prepared to make a getaway yet. I had about four hundred dollars in my bank account that I had saved up over the previous five years. The people I worked for knew I wasn't allowed to keep my own money, so at Christmas time and on my birthdays they gave me ten or fifteen dollars as a gift. I also saved most of my allowance. I had been adding to my savings account more often since June had called me at the Snyders'. I tried not to feel guilty when I skimmed several dollars off before handing my wages to Mem.

As the sun set, sending a chill over the woods, I vowed that I would leave, but I would do it in a way that would not put my safety or well-being in jeopardy.

Where would I go?

I closed my eyes. Where would I want to live, if I could live anywhere?

My eyes opened wide when the answer came. I could make my dream of living in Vermont come true. Instead of waking and finding myself back in my own bed, in Mem and Datt's house, I could really be there. I could see Mount Mansfield and Lake Champlain for real, not just pictures of them. I could sit by the waterfall beside the red covered bridge, just like the woman in the magazine.

But how would I get there?

I had always wanted to travel by train. But how would I get to the train station?

I thought of Megan. Maybe she would help me leave.

Where would I live?

Then I remembered what a woman I'd worked for once had told me when she was talking about leaving her husband. She had said that there were YWCA programs that helped women in transition.

Were there any YWCAs in Vermont?

I could find out.

It was dark now, really dark. And cold.

Should I tell Sarah or Susan in case one of them would want to come with me?

I decided to think about it.

Nearby in the darkness, leaves rustled. It was probably a raccoon going out to feed on the corn at the edge of the field. Still, it made me uneasy. I took some comfort in the fact that there were no wolves or bears or coyotes in our woods. But it could be Datt, waiting to grab me. I sat motionless, listening. The rustle did not come again.

Long after dark, I wrapped my plan like a present, tucked it away deep inside me, and slipped quietly into the basement. The house was still. It was Saturday night and I needed to take a shower, so I heated water on the oil stove as quietly as I could, mixed it with cold in the garden sprinkling can, and hung the can of water on the nail on the ceiling. I sponged down my body, then let the warm water flow down over me. I dried off, wrapped myself in towels, tiptoed up the stairs, slid into my nightdress, and then climbed into the already warm bed next to Sarah. I sighed, thinking at least I could sleep in since the next day was our "in-between-church Sunday." I was surprised as I settled in that there had been no ambush. I fell asleep quickly and easily.

Freedom lies in being bold.
ROBERT FROST

Out of the Woods

arah and Susan stood over the bed, telling me to get up. I put my head back in my pillow. I was glad I didn't need to listen to them.

"Lomie, you have to get up! Mem and Datt said so!" Susan said urgently.

I opened my eyes.

Sarah really woke me up when she said, "If you don't get up, we are going to tell Mem you called the social workers."

I sat up and glared at them. "You promised you wouldn't! That would only make things worse around here!"

"You made it worse yesterday by talking to Datt in an angry voice!" Susan said. "And then you made it even worse by not coming home! That's why you have to get up now."

"Why? Is Datt the owner of anger around here?" I asked.

"What do you mean?"

"He can get angry and hit us any time he wants, but we can't even use an angry voice?"

"He was in a good mood until you set him off. If he gets triggered, it will be your fault," Susan said.

"Whose side are you on?" I asked. "Why is it a terrible thing if you get chased out in the cold with nothing on, but all my fault if I do?"

"I didn't provoke him!" Susan snapped.

"I thought we were going to stick together," I said. I looked them square in the face—first Sarah, then Susan.

They were both silent. Then Sarah said, "We just want what's best for this family. We are going to go downstairs. If you aren't down there in ten minutes, we'll tell Mem that you called the social workers."

With that, Sarah and Susan went downstairs.

I got up and dressed slowly. So much for asking them if they wanted to go with me! Anger was taking over where sadness usually lived.

Susan had sneaked out of the house many times—and we'd covered up for her. Sarah had snuck out the window when Datt had forbidden her to go out—and we hadn't told.

Now they were being so righteous! I got up and combed the front of my hair and put my white *kopp* on. I thought, *Yes, we women and girls have to wear a covering over our heads to show that we are submissive to our men—all because God made Adam before Eve. At least that's what the men say. They like to make these rules and pretend God did.*

I put my dress on and pricked myself with a straight pin. I thought, *Stupid things! Men get to wear buttons on their shirts and we have to wear pins because buttons might be too fancy for women. Too fancy, indeed! It's only because the men are the ones making the rules.*

I went down the stairs and opened the door. There, at the round oak table, sat Datt with his big black Bible open in front of him. Next to him was Mem, and beside her were Sarah and Susan, sharing a German Testament. Simon and Katherine sat in their places in silence, with downcast eyes. There was an empty spot with an open Testament. As I stood there surveying the scene, they all looked at me like a room full of judges.

Mem said, "Sit down."

I thought about not. But there were so many of them, and only one of me. For a minute I wished I had gone out to the highway the night before.

I sat down with a tight place in my throat. Mem said, "We are going to read scriptures before breakfast this morning."

I glared across the table at Sarah and Susan. They were the same two people who a year ago had checked out a book from the library about sign language and learned how to communicate silently with one another. That was at the time when Datt would have us get on our knees for prayers every night. He would read one prayer after another, with us on our knees for sometimes more than twenty minutes. Sarah, Susan, and I knew this was another method he used to control us. This was one of the things we couldn't openly disobey, because to the rest of the community Datt was doing the right thing, praying with his family every night. Sarah and Susan used their sign language to poke fun at him. Mem had interrupted Datt to tell him what Sarah and Susan were doing. To our surprise, Datt didn't become violent. But he prayed even longer that night.

Now Sarah and Susan were helping use scripture to bring me under Datt's control? I knew they were traitors. I would certainly not tell them I was leaving!

When it was my turn to read a verse in German, I sat there for a minute. Mem said, "Lomie," in that solid voice that carried in it both her expectation and her warning. I read in a sloppy way. For once I didn't care what I was reading, or what it meant. I wanted to get through it.

The reading went on just long enough for them to feel that I had submitted, and therefore they had established their dominance over me.

After I had eaten, I slipped back into the woods and tried to figure out how to get to a phone to call Megan. I couldn't go to the Haddocks or the Gingeriches, because they'd tell Mem. The Carters let us use their phone sometimes when they weren't home, but only for emergencies. They had moved in next door when our other neighbors moved to Texas. I had seen the Carters leave while we were still reading scriptures.

But they had pet elkhounds in the house. If the dogs weren't all in their cages, they might not let me in. I would have to open the green metal door they left unlocked and go through the dark and damp basement. If the Carters came home and caught me, I would have trouble explaining what the emergency was.

I took the chance. I got through the basement, leaving the door open for light and a way to get back out. The pack of dogs all began barking when I came in. I went up the stairs. I carefully opened the door. They were all penned. The strong animal odor overwhelmed me, making it hard to breathe.

I held my breath as I reached for the phone. I waited for the dogs to stop barking, then dialed Megan's number with my heart beating faster with each ring.

At last there was a click, then Megan's voice said, "Hello?"

"Hello, Megan? This is Saloma."

"Hi, Saloma, what's up?" She sounded cheerful and normal, with no idea what I was about to ask her.

I drew a deep breath. "I was wondering if you would help me leave home," I said. Then I waited. After a pause, I added, "Things have gotten worse."

She didn't ask me any questions.

"Of course I will," she said calmly. "Where are you now?"

"I'm at the neighbors."

"Do they know what you are doing?"

"No, they aren't home. They said we could use the phone in emergencies."

"Uh-oh, what if they come home? We'd better plan fast. Can you come to my house?"

"Yes," I said.

"All right," she said. "Don't come directly to my house. I will pick you up in front of the drugstore in the mall. Do you know where I mean?"

"Yes."

"Good. When would you like to do this?"

Right now, I wanted to say. "Whenever it's good for you."

"The Tuesday after next, I am getting ready for my sister to arrive from France. How about Tuesday of the following week? Maybe you could babysit the children when my sister is here."

"That's fine," I said, wondering how I would survive another nine days.

"Okay, I'll see you then," Megan said.

I hung up. Before I could begin to grasp the enormity of what I'd just done, the dogs began barking again. I heard the key in the door click, and then Denise walked in.

She looked surprised to see me. "What is going on?" she asked.

To my surprise, my voice sounded normal. "I hope you don't mind, but I needed to use a phone. It was a local call."

"Is everything okay?" she asked.

I knew I couldn't say there was an emergency. So I lied. "Yes. I was in a pinch with arrangements for work. I had a mix-up."

"I don't mind you using the phone, but I'd rather you do it when I'm here, unless it's an emergency."

"I'm sorry," I said. I added, "It won't happen again."

CHURCH WAS AT THE YODERS' my last church Sunday, which was a five-mile walk, one way. I walked with Sarah and Susan. Usually I tried to talk to them, but during the past few months, they would give me the cold shoulder and berate me for talking too much, for the way I walked, the way I waved, or for anything else they could find fault with. On this Sunday, I walked with them in silence, lost in a world of my own. I was thinking, *I am about to attend my last Amish church service.*

Sarah interrupted my thoughts. "So Lomie, why are you so quiet today?"

Susan said, "Yeah, I didn't think you could be this quiet. Did the cat bite your tongue?"

I decided not to respond.

When we got to church, Sarah and Susan made as if they were best friends with each other and not related to me. I didn't care. I looked around and wondered if I would miss anyone there. I didn't think I would. I wondered if anyone would miss me. I didn't think they would.

The singing at church was nice that day, and I joined in. As soon as the first preacher stood up, I crossed my arms over my knees and put my head down on my arms, the way I usually did to sleep and tune out the preachers. It was common for people to fall asleep now and again. But I did it deliberately, every time. It was my way of avoiding the inner conflict I often felt when I didn't agree with what the preachers said.

This time I used it as a way of having privacy for my thoughts about what I would be doing in two days. That is, if Sarah and Susan didn't discover my plan and tell on me, and I could actually follow through with it. If they told on me, I would be overwhelmed with people talking me out of it—the bishop, the ministers, uncles and aunts, neighbors, and most especially Joe and the rest of the family. I knew if I made it, I could not tell anyone where I was. If I did, the letters and phone calls from people trying to convince me to come back would be overpowering. I wondered if they would send a van-load of people all the way to Vermont to pick me up, as they had done to a young woman in Aunt Lizzie's community in Pennsylvania who had run away.

Or maybe they would be glad to get rid of a troublemaker like me.

ON THE WAY HOME, Sarah and Susan acted differently towards me. They seemed to be testing me to see if my new resolve to be quiet was temporary or not. But no matter how hard they tried to draw me out, I kept my secret hidden deep inside me. I walked alongside my sisters while remaining alone and private.

When we got home, we popped corn, and then our boyfriends came. When Dan walked into my room, part way through the afternoon, I realized this might be the last time I would see him. I felt guilty that my plan didn't include telling him face-to-face that I didn't want to go steady with him anymore. But I sensed that would be a very difficult thing to do, and I had already decided to kill two birds with one stone by leaving the Amish and him at the same time.

"Dan," I said that evening while we were sitting on the edge of my bed, "do you want to go to the singing tonight?"

"Well, I suppose we could. I'm a little concerned about the distance my horse would have to go, though."

I remembered Joe using that excuse when Emma wanted to go to a singing and he didn't.

"We don't have to; I was just thinking it would be nice for a change. It's been awhile since we've gone," I said. I was also thinking how it would be my last one, but I kept that thought quiet.

"How about next week? We've been invited to my friend Eddie's for supper, remember? There's going to be a bunch of us, and then a singing afterwards."

I remembered. I regretted that I wouldn't get a chance to see Eddie again. "That would be fine," I said, thinking that maybe his horse would have more pep the following week. Then I wondered if he would still go, once he found out about me being gone.

That is, if I made it.

I ASKED MEM IF SHE would split the taxi fare to Middlefield on Monday. She said yes. She went to Spector's store to buy material for a dress, and I walked immediately to the bank and withdrew the contents of my savings account. With the money I had skimmed off the earnings I gave Mem and Datt, and the savings, I had $450 to make this journey. Then I went to the dime store and bought new underwear. I knew I would be buying "high" clothes later, but I figured I might as well buy my underwear in a familiar place, because that would be one thing I wouldn't need to change. It felt comforting that I would be changing on the outside, but inside I would really still be the same.

When I got home, I walked to the mailbox. An autumn breeze caught my dress and blew it against my legs. Oak leaves lifted and circled in a little eddy, then floated back down to the ground. I was so excited, I felt like one of those leaves. By this time tomorrow, I could dance in a circle just like those leaves, and no one would be there to criticize me.

I thought more about my name. I would have to change it. Saloma would stand out too much. I had narrowed my choices—Heidi, Maria, Julia, or Linda. I had always wanted Sue for a middle name. Not only had I gotten an old-fashioned Amish name when I was born, but Datt's mother didn't believe in middle names, so none of us got any. Now I could name myself anything I wanted.

Lamb's wool clouds floated in the sky above the neighbors' field. I looked up and drew strength from the blue around them. Malinda Sue Miller. I liked it. I could see myself fitting into that name. Julia or Maria were too glamorous for me.

I went upstairs and packed my little blue overnight suitcase as full as I could with my underwear and slips. I put my money into a pocket on the inside of the suitcase, along with my comb and brush, and a few dozen pictures that Joe and Sarah had taken with a camera they'd had on the sly, a long time ago. Then I hid the packed suitcase in my closet behind my dresses.

I couldn't sleep all night. I tried not to toss and turn or wake Sarah, who was sleeping in the same bed. I kept thinking about the little suitcase only a few feet away, behind the closet door. I played the scene in my mind over and over. I'd wait in my room, in my gray dress, coat, white scarf, and boots until Mr. Pell drove into the lane. Mem would certainly announce when he came. Then by the sound of her voice, I would know whether she was in the living room or the kitchen. If she was in the living room, I would go quickly through the kitchen and out the door before she discovered I had a suitcase in my hand. If she was in the kitchen, I would tell her I was babysitting overnight at the place where I worked. This would also give me the extra day I needed to get out of town before anyone found out that I was gone.

I got up earlier than usual, but not so early that anyone would suspect. The yellow car drove in. Mem announced it from the kitchen. I went quickly down the stairs and came face to face with her. She was sweeping around the table, but she stopped and looked pointedly at the suitcase in my hand.

"I'm babysitting tonight at the place where I work."

Mem looked at me hard, then at the suitcase, and realized she had no choice in this one. "Well, just don't let it happen too often."

"I won't," I said. I went quickly down the steps and out the door before she could call me back.

As Mr. Pell drove out the driveway past the kitchen window, I saw Mem looking out at me. Without thinking about it, my hand went up and I gave her a wave. I wondered if I would ever see her again. I knew it would be really hard for her when she found out that I had left. I also knew that if I started feeling sorry for Mem, I would not be able to leave. The car kept going. I was not running away blindly, I told myself. I had made plans and had money. I would be all right.

Mr. Pell wanted to drive me to wherever I was going to be working that day, but I insisted he drop me off in front of the drugstore. He did that after saying for the second time, "I can drive you right to work, like I usually do."

"No, that's okay. I will be doing some shopping," I said.

I was early. I went into a shoe store and bought a pair of beige shoes. Then I went into the drugstore next door and bought a pair of pantyhose. The clerks gave me strange looks. I said nothing to explain myself.

Megan arrived with her station wagon full of children. She looked amazed that I was really there with a suitcase. I got in for the short ride to her house, and I was relieved that she said nothing about having changed her mind about wanting to help me. As soon as we got to her home, she sent the children to the playroom and we started planning.

"You did it!" she said. "You left! What was it like this morning? Do they have any idea?"

I didn't want to talk about it. Briefly, I told her what I'd told Mem about babysitting overnight, and then I said that the first thing I wanted to do was cut my hair.

"Is that necessary?" she asked. "Many women have long hair."

"My hair looks like a horse's tail when it's down," I said, "because I've been putting it up in barrettes and it is all broken."

"Why don't you go up and take a shower, and when your hair dries, I will take a look at it."

Megan took one look at my hair when it was down, and she said, "You are right, it does look like a horse's tail." She picked up the phone and made an appointment at her hairdresser's that afternoon. "We can take you clothes shopping afterwards," she said. "Now, do you have any idea where you want to go when you leave?"

"I want to go to Vermont," I said.

"Oh? Do you know someone there?"

"No."

"Then why Vermont?"

"It's where I've always wanted to go, so I figured since I'm running away, I may as well go to someplace I like."

"How do you know about Vermont?" Megan asked.

"I remember reading about it and seeing pictures in geography books in school."

Megan looked at me with a sideways smile on her face.

"I also have been getting *Vermont Life* magazines," I said.

She laughed.

"You don't think that's a good idea?" I asked.

"No, I think it's fine. I am just amazed that you are so clear about this. So, how will you get there?"

"I was thinking of taking a train, if there are connections."

"Where in Vermont do you want to go?"

"I heard about YWCA places that house women in transition. I want to find out where in Vermont they might be located. I'd rather live in the country than a city."

"We could call the Vermont Chamber of Commerce. But some YWCAs don't have rooms for rent, so be sure to ask them if they do," Megan said.

"How am I going to pay you for the call?"

"You may use my phone as much as you need to and I will pay for it. That will be my gift to you," Megan said.

"I don't know how I will ever thank you. I couldn't be doing this at all without your help."

"I'm glad you called me," Megan said with a genuine smile.

First I called information to get the number for the Vermont Chamber of Commerce. I called them and asked where in Vermont they had YWCAs that housed women. The woman I spoke to said there was one in Rutland

and one in Burlington. Then she double-checked that and said the only one that was a residential YWCA in all of Vermont was in Burlington. She gave me that phone number.

Next, I called the Y and talked to Mrs. Ohr, the director there. She said there was a room available for a week. I asked if there was anything available after that, and she said something might become available. It would cost eight dollars a week. I made reservations for a week, beginning the next day.

Next, I called the train station and asked for the cost of a one-way ticket to Burlington, Vermont. The ticket agent said the best way to get to Burlington was to take the train to Port Kent, New York, on the other side of Lake Champlain from Burlington, then take a ferry across the lake. I said that sounded fine. I booked a ticket for the next night, leaving the city at 11:20 P.M. The ticket cost forty dollars.

After lunch, Megan took me to have my hair cut. The salon was a small but bright shop off the main street, and the man who greeted us at the door took us to a station in the far back. I took off my *kopp* and pulled my hair free of the barrettes and pins that held it up. The man made no comment about the gray Amish dress I was wearing; all he seemed to be aware of was my hair.

"What have you been doing to your hair?" he asked as soon as I'd sat down in a padded chair.

"Putting it up in barrettes," I said faintly.

"But what about this?" he asked. He picked up the broken strands of hair in a circle around my head where my covering had hidden it up until now.

"I've been using a rubber band as a hair band."

"You should never use a rubber band in your hair. You can see, right here," and he picked up the strands, "where you broke the hair and it's all frizzy. Now you are going to need to grow it all out before it's going to look healthy again."

"I won't use rubber bands anymore," I promised.

"How much do you want me to cut?" he asked.

"I'd like it to be as long as possible, but still have it look good."

He shook his head slowly. "I'm going to need to cut at least up to this point." He laid his finger across my hair, just below my shoulders.

My hair was the length of my back.

I gulped, and then told him to go ahead and cut it. As he snipped and the horse's tail fell to the floor, all I could think about was the Bible verse that said it was a sin for a woman to be shorn and shaven.

That's how I felt when he was done: shorn and shaven. But it was only one of the many sins I committed that day.

That night, I lay in a single bed in one of the children's rooms, and I couldn't sleep. I kept feeling my hair, loose on the pillow around me. I kept thinking about the clothing lying on the chair beside the bed. I had bought a green wool skirt and jacket, and a cream-colored turtleneck top to go with it. I had paid over twenty-five dollars for the outfit. That left a little less than four hundred dollars for my journey.

I still worried that I would not be able to leave before I was found out. Mem and my sisters did not know where I was working that day, and it would be the following evening before they would know I was gone.

In the dim light of the nightlight in the hallway, I tossed and turned. I got a fluttering feeling in my stomach. I couldn't tell if it came from fear, excitement, or both. I finally fell asleep in the darkest hours of early morning.

The following day, Megan told me that she wanted her husband, Peter, to have a talk with me about what to do and what not to do while I was traveling. She herded the children out of the kitchen, and Peter sat across the table from me. I felt self-conscious as he gave me all the "don'ts." "If a man wants you to go with him to his apartment, don't go. If a guy talks to you and you feel uncomfortable, tell him to leave you alone."

I had thought I would go by my own instincts, but now I was wondering if they would be reliable. Peter made me feel as though there might be more "bad guys" out in the world than I had thought.

Megan wanted me to write to Mem to let her know I was all right. I wanted to leave and not have any way for them to know where I was. But on the other hand, I didn't want them to think I'd been kidnapped. So I let Megan talk me into writing a short note that said: "I'm writing to you to let you know I am all right. I'm leaving because of Datt's violence. I can't live like this anymore. You had the chance to get help for him, and you didn't. I will not be coming back until he does get help, so don't try to find me."

I didn't add that I wouldn't be coming back even if he did get help. I asked Megan to mail my letter the next day, so that I would have left town before Mem got it.

That evening, Megan's sister and her husband arrived from France. Megan had told me that her sister and her husband were very wealthy, and I realized from the way she talked that she wanted very much to make a good impression on them.

My job was to keep the children occupied while Megan, Peter, and the esteemed sister and her husband ate dinner in the dining room with the door closed.

I put the children to bed at eight o'clock. Then I took a shower, combed my shorn hair and pinned it back with barrettes, got dressed in my new clothes, and packed a white suitcase that Megan had given me, which was bigger than the one I'd brought from home. She gave me several sweaters and other pieces of clothing. I felt bareheaded as I walked downstairs into the living room with a suitcase in each hand.

Peter looked at me and his eyes sparkled. "Well, Saloma, I must say you look very attractive and pretty."

"Thank you," I said. I could feel myself blushing. I wasn't used to compliments about my appearance.

We started out for the station early and got there in plenty of time. Peter waited with me, even though I told him if he wanted to go back home to their company, I would be fine.

I purchased the ticket, then stood on the platform with Peter, waiting for the train. When it pulled in, Peter handed me an envelope and said it wasn't much, but it was his and Megan's way of wishing me well.

"Oh, thank you," I said, meaning it sincerely. "You've already helped me out so much. I can't ever repay you for all you and Megan have done."

Peter gave me a good-bye hug and kissed me in a way that made me focus quickly on picking up my two suitcases and boarding the train. His hand lingered on my back. I was completely confused. Peter, who had warned me about men with bad intentions, had given me a kiss like that—on the lips?

It made me realize something about "high" people I hadn't known before. My Amish clothes and appearance had been a shield, and without it, I was vulnerable. It seemed to me that Peter had been the first one to take advantage of my shield being gone. Would there be others? As I stepped up into the train, I wondered what was getting myself into.

When you do things from your soul you feel a river moving in you, a joy.
RUMI

Into Daybreak

hen I saw how crowded the train was, I forgot the kiss and focused on finding a seat. All of the double seats had at least one person in them, except one. That one had a pack on it. I decided to take my chances. I put my luggage on the rack above and scooted into the seat next to the pack.

A tall man stopped in the aisle beside me. He had thin blond hair with a tinge of red, and a balding spot on the crown of his head. Despite the bald spot, he looked like he might be in his late twenties.

"Were you sitting here?" I asked him.

"Yes, but you are welcome to take this seat next to mine," he said.

I let him into the seat by the window.

"I'm John," he said.

"My name is Linda," I said. "Linda Sue Miller." I said it with such confidence, anyone listening would have never guessed this was the first day I had the name.

"Hello, Linda," he answered.

Just then, the train began to move. My heart pounded to the beat of the wheels on the rail. I stood up and waved to Peter, and he waved back, and then he and the platform were gone, and the train picked up speed and rushed into the darkness. Everything swayed and vibrated, and the feeling entered my bones. I liked the train already.

"Is he your father?" John asked.

"No," I said, sitting back down. "Just a friend."

"Where are you traveling to?"

"I'm going to Burlington, Vermont," I said, half expecting him to be surprised.

But he just said, "I'm going to Boston to visit a few friends of mine. We usually get together about once every six months. I haven't seen them in a while, so I'm going there for the week. How long will you be in Burlington?"

"I don't know yet." There was a long pause.

John looked at me, expecting me to clarify.

I suddenly felt so relieved to have made it onto the train, on the way to freedom, I decided to take the chance that my instincts were right, that this man was trustworthy. I said softly, "I'm running away from home."

John got a surprised look on his face, as his mouth formed an O.

"Not only am I leaving my family, I am also leaving the Amish," I said.

John looked twice as surprised. "Wow. That must take a lot of courage," he said.

I shrugged and nodded.

He smiled and said, "I have had some contact with Amish folks. I'm an intern at the Children's Hospital, and occasionally there are Amish children who need care from us."

I hoped he wouldn't mention our conversation to any Amish people.

"So, what prompts you to leave?" he asked.

The story flowed out from me naturally, like water over rocks in a brook. I told him about Datt, about my brothers and sisters, about my love of Vermont, and why I finally decided to leave.

"This really must take a lot of courage for you," John said again.

"Not really. I think running away from my problems is less courageous than sticking it out at home."

"It sounds like it was intolerable for you, though."

"It was." I kept my voice even. I was aware of having no covering on my head, and a skirt that didn't cover my knees when I sat down. I couldn't believe I was talking so intimately with a stranger.

John and I talked for a long time. I found myself combing my hair with my fingers and pulling strands of hair away from my neck. At some point, I said I should get some rest, since the last few nights I'd hardly slept. He said, "You are welcome to lean against me if you want to."

"Oh, no, that's okay," I said, shifting my body away from his.

"Okay, that's fine," he said. I could tell he wasn't offended. I sensed it would have been fine, yet I remembered the tone of Peter's talk and decided it was probably best that I had the reaction I did.

We had been quiet for a few minutes when the conductor came and offered me a seat by myself in the car up ahead. I followed him, telling John I would be back in the morning to get my luggage.

The double seat by myself felt lonely. The train car was filled with people sleeping. I looked out at the dark November landscape and felt cold. Signs in a town we went through told me we'd crossed into New York State. I wished I had one of the sweaters Megan had given me, but it was in my suitcase. Then I noticed other people had blankets and pillows, and I wondered where they had gotten them. Soon, the conductor came by with one of each and offered them to me. I thanked him and leaned up against the window.

Tonight Mem would know that I was gone. I wondered if she was sitting in the living room under the hissing of the Coleman lantern, crying into her handkerchief. Or was she moving towards her bedroom in the flickering light of the lantern after she had turned it off, before it died out completely? I was glad I was safely on the train, with no turning back, and that I wouldn't be there to see Mem cry. Then I realized for the first time in my life that possibly Mem brought some of her sorrow on herself. I couldn't keep going on this journey if I was going to feel sorry for her.

I wondered whether they would let Dan know I was gone, once they got my letter. Or would they tell him when he came to visit me on Sunday afternoon? Then I reminded myself that by the next day, the news would be all over the community. I was relieved to think I didn't have to be with Dan ever again, and I didn't have to "tell him off," as the Amish called breaking up with someone. I don't know how I could have told him, given the way he didn't want to talk about anything personal.

I realized I had talked with John about more personal things in a few hours than I had with Dan in the five months I'd known him.

Somewhere in my turmoil of thoughts, I drifted into the place between waking and dreaming, where thoughts and dreams mix together.

When I awoke, the train was traveling into a red morning sun above the brown November fields. I thought about Datt's saying, "Red sky in the morning is a sailor's warning."

I wondered if Datt was in his bent hickory rocking chair in the living room on the woven rug, with the sun coming through the east windows. Was he yawning loudly, or did he do that only when I was there because he knew it bothered me? Was Mem up, starting the fire in the cookstove in the kitchen, getting ready to make breakfast?

I looked out into the morning for a long time. What would it be like in Burlington, Vermont? Would the people be friendly? What would I do for work? Where would I live if I could only stay one week at the YWCA?

I was feeling hungry and thirsty. I wished I had a cold glass of orange juice. I wondered what time it was, and I decided to go visit John. I hoped he was awake. I walked through the door at the end of my car, across the little metal bridge between cars, trying not to look at the tracks rushing by underneath through the gap in the floors, then into John's car. He was sitting with his head back and his eyes closed. I thought about going back to my seat, but that was too lonely. I decided to go and get my luggage from the rack above him.

John opened his eyes when I reached up into the rack. He seemed surprised and sleepy. I apologized for disturbing him and offered to get the suitcases later, but he said, "No, that's fine. Would you like to sit down for a bit?"

"Sure," I said and sat down much too quickly. John looked a bit startled and blinked a few times to wake up. "I can come back later," I said as I started to get up.

"No it's fine, really. I'm awake."

He got an orange out of his pack and offered me some slices. I took them. They were juicy and sweet. But it wasn't as easy to talk to him as it had been earlier, so when we got close to Albany where I would switch trains, I said good-bye to him. He offered me his address and said he would like to hear how things were going for me. I accepted it and assured him I would write. I took my luggage and went back to my seat.

I had a five-hour wait in Albany. I thought about going to a store to shop for clothes, but I was afraid I would get lost. I stayed in the station and tried to sleep on a hard, white plastic chair. But I was afraid that I would miss my train, and every time I dozed off, I would jump awake again. After several hours passed, I walked restlessly around the station, bought a hamburger, and finally boarded a train in mid-afternoon, bound for Port Kent.

The conductor shook his head in puzzlement at my ticket. As I sat down, I heard him mumble something about "Port Kent?" and he gave me a strange look. I wondered if he knew I was a runaway.

The train began moving. I breathed more easily. Surely if he was going to report me, he wouldn't have done anything to show that he was suspicious.

I had a full seat to myself this time, and I relaxed into the swaying and vibrating. Even though I was tired, I felt my confidence building. I had gotten through the train switch all by myself, as though I'd done it many times. I could do this.

Then, just as I was starting to feel relaxed and sleepy at last, the conductor came by and asked to check my ticket again. I gave it to him. He stuck it up in the rack above my head and walked down the aisle, shaking his head and muttering under his breath, "Port Kent . . . Port Kent . . ."

Two women from across the aisle looked at me. "Why is he so worried about your ticket?" one of them asked me.

Maybe because I'm a runaway, I felt like saying. But I just shrugged and said I didn't know. They fussed and said they thought he should leave me alone —that I was very well-dressed for a young woman, and that there were few young women who dressed this way anymore. To take the focus off of me, I asked them where they were traveling to, and they said they were just coming home from being on the *Phil Donahue Show* the day before. I had often watched that show while I was cleaning.

The train began traveling through mountains that were covered with a carpet of freshly fallen leaves beneath bare trees. As dusk was gathering, the occasional whistle from the train made me think of Hank Williams's haunting voice singing, *I'm so lonesome I could cry* . . . It had been one of my favorite songs when I listened to country music on the radio at the houses I cleaned. I'd wait to run the vacuum cleaner if a song by Hank Williams came on the radio.

The dark mountains loomed above and around the train as it curved through the valleys. Partly because I wanted to talk to someone, but mostly because I wanted to know, I stopped the conductor when he walked by and asked him what mountains we were going through.

"The Adirondacks," he answered. He looked at me for a minute. Then he blurted out, "I don't mean to be rude, but what *are* you going to do in Port Kent? That is a nothing place with no phones, no restaurants, and no places to stay. It is only a stop on the tracks in the middle of the woods!"

I didn't know whether to be relieved or scared. "The ticket agent in Ohio told me I could take a ferry across the lake to Burlington, Vermont, from Port Kent. She said I could walk to the ferry ramp from the train stop."

He shook his head soberly. "That ferry was discontinued twelve days ago."

It was dark out now. I couldn't see the mountains anymore. I imagined myself getting off the train, stranded in the dark woods with my two suitcases. It felt as though someone had dropped something heavy in the bottom of my stomach.

"So how can I get to Burlington?" I asked.

"If you want to get there by train, you would have to go up to Montreal in Canada, then back down to Essex Junction in Vermont," he said.

"How much would that cost?" I asked.

"I don't know. I could find out for you. But wait a minute; there is a couple at the end of the car who have tickets for Port Kent. Let me ask them if they're going to Vermont."

"I would be glad to pay for a ride," I said.

"Just a minute; I'll ask," the conductor said. He approached an elderly couple, and I heard him ask if they were going to Burlington.

The woman nodded.

"How are you getting there from Port Kent?" he asked.

"Our daughter," the woman said in a foreign accent.

"There is a young woman on the train who needs a ride to Burlington. Would you give her one? She is willing to pay for gas."

"No! No! Can't do that, she's a stranger!" said the woman, shaking her head.

"She is a very nice young lady, and she doesn't have a way to get to Burlington . . ."

"No, no, can't do that, she's a stranger," she repeated.

The conductor came back to me and said, "Have your luggage ready and we'll just see." As he spoke, he used the same tone of voice and choice of words that Olin Clara had often used.

I was standing in the aisle with my suitcases in hand when the train stopped and the door opened. A woman called, "Hi Mom! Hi Dad!" and began helping the older couple down the train steps. The conductor leaned out the door and said, "There's a young woman on the train who needs a ride to Burlington. Will you give her one?"

"Sure, come along!" said the daughter with a welcoming wave of her arm.

"Go! Go!" the conductor said, nearly pushing me from the train and handing me my two suitcases. Then the door closed and the train moved on down the tracks.

I looked at the tall trees and dark woods around me. I had no choice but to follow the family down the driveway to the little white car parked there. The mother was saying, "You can't do that; she's a stranger!"

"Oh Mom, I'm a Vermonter!" said the daughter as she opened the trunk of her car and put in her parents' luggage. She gestured for me to do the same.

"You can sit in the back," she said, and I climbed in next to her mother and her eight-year-old son, who looked at me in wide-eyed silence.

"So, what are you going to do in Vermont?" the daughter asked me as she started driving.

"I—I don't know," I said, feeling the same panic setting in that I'd felt at first with John. Here I was, surrounded by strangers in a strange car on a strange road. I wished that lying came naturally to me. "I'm leaving home. I'm going to stay at the YWCA and find work."

"See, I told you!" the mother snapped. "Now you've got a runaway in your car!"

"Oh mother," the woman said, laughing nervously. To my relief, she didn't ask me any more questions. I saw her holding hands with her father in silence.

I kept quiet. We drove through the woods until we came to a ferry crossing between Essex, New York, and Charlotte, Vermont.

I couldn't enjoy the ride on the water. It had sounded romantic, entering Vermont for the first time by ferry on Lake Champlain at night, but it was more scary than romantic. While the daughter wasn't driving, I insisted on giving her ten dollars. She didn't want to take any money. Then she asked, "How about five dollars?" I insisted on ten.

At last, we drove down Main Street in Burlington, where big houses lined the road. I watched for number 278. I saw Lake Champlain, looking dark in the distance beyond the buildings.

The daughter asked, "Mom, would you like to go to McDonald's?"

"No, get rid of her first!" the mother said.

The daughter shook her head with a resigned sigh and pulled into the short driveway of the old brick building at 278. She got out and helped me with my luggage. "I am so sorry about my mother," she said."

"I'm sorry for you. Looks like I've made your visit with your parents difficult."

"Don't you worry. It would've happened anyway. When my brother put them on the train in California, he warned them not to talk to strangers. I think my mother has taken that too far. Please call me when you can. I'd like to know how you're doing. My name is Sprite and I'm in the phone book."

I said I would. Then I walked up the old wooden steps and rang the front doorbell of the YWCA. I was so hungry and weary I could hardly think anymore.

A woman came to the door and let me in. With a pleasant smile, she introduced herself as Annabelle, told me she had one of the rooms upstairs, and showed me to a room behind the back staircase, next to the kitchen. It was small, with a faded gray carpet on the floor. But it was all mine, and for that reason it might as well have been a room in a mansion. I finally had a room of my own! I stretched out on the single bed with my clothes on and felt as though I didn't want to move again. All I could think about was that the clock I'd noticed in the kitchen said it was 9:10, and how exactly twenty-four hours earlier, I'd been taking a shower in Megan and Peter's house.

Annabelle had said the housemother would be there soon. Before long, I heard several women coming into the kitchen. I got up off the bed and combed my hair, pinned it back again with barrettes, then entered the kitchen. Maureen, the housemother, was about my age, with long red hair and mischievous eyes. She introduced me to Bernice, a tall, thin woman. Bernice and Annabelle were having toast, and they offered me some. I asked about food arrangements, and they told me that everyone was in charge of her own. We had designated shelves in the cupboard and refrigerator.

The girls wanted to know where I was from and how I had gotten there. I told them my story. All three of them were spellbound. As soon as I had finished, the questions began.

"How did you get here?"

"Why did you pick Vermont?"

"How did you know about this Y?"

"You only went through eighth grade? I would never have guessed, you speak so well." After nearly an hour had passed, Maureen asked, "So what are you going to do now?"

"First I'd like to find out if I can stay here longer than one week," I said.

"Of course," she answered. "The director isn't going to put you out on the street. You can apply for permanent residency and you can stay as long as you want to."

"That's a relief," I said. "As to what I will do for work: I'd love to be a waitress, but I have only cleaned houses. I might have to start with that."

"Do you have a social security number?"

"No, I don't."

"You will need one before you can get a full-time job. The social security office is right on Pearl Street, downtown. I can give you directions."

"What about clothes?" I asked. "Is there a second-hand shop? I don't have too much money, but I do need clothes. These are the only ones I bought in Ohio. I'm going to need a winter coat."

Annabelle said, "There's a shop called "Second Hand Rose" right next to the social security office. I'm going down to Pearl Street tomorrow, so I can take you there."

"Oh, thank you," I said. "I'm not used to finding my way around a city."

"This is not like a huge city. You can find your way around easily. You'll get used to it very quickly," Maureen said.

"I also want to go back to school," I said.

"Well, there is a great work-study program at a place called the Church Street Center. You could probably do work in exchange for courses," Bernice said.

"Oh, that sounds perfect for me," I said.

"You are going to have so much fun," Maureen said, as she gave me a mischievous sideways grin. I wondered if she would be a bad influence on me. I felt that I would need to balance the wonderful feeling of my newfound freedom with common sense to remain clear about who I was as a person.

I smiled back and said, "I know it!"

Everyone became quiet for a minute. Then Annabelle said, "I will show you where the bed linens and towels are."

I made my bed, then ran a deep bath in a tub with claw feet in the bathroom above the back stairs. As I lay in the bath, deep enough to cover my whole body, I wondered what was going on back home.

Joe would probably be there, telling Mem and Datt, "Don't worry, she will come back," in his self-assured way. I liked the feeling of Joe not knowing where I was, any more than any of the rest of them. For the first time in my life, he had no control over me.

I felt sorry that Sarah and Susan had to see Mem's sorrow and Datt's anger. Would Datt believe them if they said they didn't know where I was, or would he think if he hit them hard enough they would have to tell? I shuddered, remembering what it felt like to have Datt storm after me. I remembered sitting in the woods, wanting to run away, and feeling as if Datt's trees were holding me in. I thought they were stronger than me, with their roots growing so deep, just as I thought the Amish traditions were strong enough to hold me in the community.

But here I am, I thought. I could hear Maureen, Bernice, and Annabelle preparing for bed. I knew I had made new friends already. It was refreshing to know people who liked to ask questions as much as I did. No one would tell me what I wasn't allowed to do tomorrow. I would decide that on my own. Maureen said I would be able to see Mount Mansfield from the top of Main Street. I would walk there and see the mountain before I went to the social security office, the clothing shop, and the grocery store.

After drying off and getting into my nightdress, I went down the stairs and into my room. I switched off the lamp and lay in my new bed. I felt both exhausted and exhilarated. I closed my eyes and thanked God for the angels along my way. I realized that I could pray and believe in God in whatever way I wanted. There was no one telling me that what I believed was wrong. Maybe people really weren't angels, but I thought about the women I had just met, of Megan and Peter, John, the conductor, and Mrs. Sprite in her little white car, and they were all angels to me. *If the Amish were right, I shouldn't be here right now. But, how could something that felt so right be wrong?* I remembered the image I had had during the three communion services I attended in the community, in which the bishop had told us the communion story about the wheat that is ground into flour and made into bread. When he asked the people in the community to give up their individuality for the sake of the community, I'd imagined that I was a grain that had fallen by the wayside and escaped the grindstone. I knew that if I had dared to tell anyone Amish about my image, they would have shamed me for my wayward thoughts. Now I hoped I was one of the wayward grains who would take root and grow.

I AWAKE SLOWLY, taking in my surroundings. Oftentimes when I awake, my first thoughts are similar to those I fell asleep with, and this morning is no exception. I love that place between sleeping and waking, when it feels as though my soul can wander freely between the two realms—that of the dream world and the waking world. I recall waking up that first morning at the Y in Burlington, Vermont, almost twenty-seven years ago, in my very own, warm room. It felt like my freedom was boundless— for the first time in my life, I did not need to live up to anyone else's expectations. It felt like I had woken up inside one of my fantasies while staring at a picture in a *Vermont Life* magazine.

When I watched David and Tim drive away from Green Street late last night, I was again amazed and grateful for the life David and I have made together. When I was with the Amish, I could never have anticipated meeting David at the Y and building a lasting relationship with him. That is yet another chapter of my journey.

I look out into the morning sun, and suddenly the parallel is obvious: waking up here by the Smith College campus, being able to chart my own path in my long-yearned-for education is just as euphoric as waking up at the Y was years ago. Though the focus is very different, I lived in a community of women then, as I do now. Here the focus is on my education, which is further along my path than when I lived at the Y. *And who would have thought,* I whisper to myself. I recall the morning in the fall when my siblings were returning to school, and I could no longer go because I had graduated from eighth grade.

When Yoxall's station wagon arrived to pick up my siblings that fall morning, I watched them eagerly heading out the lane. I longed to go back to school so badly that I could smell the books that had been stored on the shelves in the entrance of the schoolhouse all summer. I could see the clean sheets of paper before I had written anything on them, leaving all possibilities open. I could feel myself running over the schoolyard, playing Hide and Seek, Softball, or Prisoner's Base, and I could hear the bell at the end of recess. When I could no longer stand the longing, I turned away from the window. Mem was waving good-bye to the others as I slipped upstairs, hoping she would think I was making my bed. Instead, I sat on it and stared at the oval crocheted rug at my feet.

What, I wondered, did I have to look forward to now? I would have to put up with the drudgery of work, work, and more work. It would have been a relief to cry as I stared at the rug, but the feelings seemed stuck in my chest. No one would understand, even if I could express my feelings. Mem was glad I wasn't going back to school; she needed my help. Lizzie was glad she didn't have to go back to school; she would scoff at me. My friends didn't long to go back to school, because they accepted the Amish ways better than I did. Mem's voice cut into my thoughts. *"Lomie, wo bischt du?"* (Lomie, where are you?)

Where do you think I am? I wanted to say. But I didn't say anything. I got up and made my bed. I went downstairs and faced the pile of breakfast dishes. Lizzie, who had a whole year of practice of working at home, was washing the dishes. I picked up a dish towel and began the hideous task of drying.

When I was fourteen and still dependent on my parents, I had to live with the Amish rule that all young people are finished with school when they graduate from eighth grade. The tradition had been in force too long to allow for exceptions, and I was too young to leave the community and make it on my own. Besides, my job at that time was to conform to the Amish ways and get ready to be a member of the church.

The most common German hymn sung in my home community is about two paths, one being narrow and the other wide. The Amish interpret this as meaning that there are only a few who take the narrow path, leading to Heaven, while the wide path leads to Hell. I do not know whether the path I took was wide or narrow, but I know that my path diverged from the one my parents chose for themselves and for me. Datt's path was often dark with sorrow and self-loathing, which spilled over into our lives, and Mem's path had left her frustrated with an unfulfilled life. Perhaps sometime in the future, now that Datt is no longer with us, Mem will share more of her inner life with me, especially that mysterious time in her young life I know so little about.

Back on that day when I was shedding my Amish clothing and having my hair cut and buying my first "English" clothing, it was as if I was transforming from a chrysalis to a butterfly. I felt like a caterpillar in my dark cocoon when I was in the community, and my subsequent freedom gave me wings—flying, as in my dream, from one adventure to another, like a butterfly floats and darts from one flower to another. Perhaps I have always believed that I would transform into exactly who and what I was meant to become.

I find that sometimes the surprises in my life are just as significant as the accomplishments I have long planned and sacrificed for. I could never have dreamed of the reconciliation I felt with my original community through Datt's funeral. Through the grace with which David, Tim, and I were received, I felt as if these people in my original community were acknowledging me for who I am for the first time in my life. I no longer felt pressure to conform to their ways. Likewise, the respect that David, Tim, and I were able to show in return hopefully conveyed to them that I wish to honor their long-held traditions.

I hear my housemates stirring, preparing themselves for a new day. I stretch and get out of bed to do the same. This morning I will attend my Scandinavian Mythology class, and this afternoon I will start catching up on my reading and homework. I look forward to dinner in the shared kitchen tonight, when I will relate my weekend adventures to my housemates.

Naming Practices among the Amish

Because the Amish don't have much variety in names, either first or last, some people have the same first and last names. Last names are not used very often (partly because it isn't that useful, with half the population being Millers, and partly because it is more formal than first names), so it becomes necessary to differentiate between one Joe Miller and another. They use the father's name first, and thus my grandfather became Mosa Joe (Mose's Joe) and my brother became Sim's (Amish for Simon's) Joe. Sometimes using the name of the father doesn't go back far enough, because there could be several Joe's Johns, for instance. So then they go back another generation to include the grandfather. That is how Milo's Mel's Dan came about (Milo's son Mel's [short for Melvin's] son, Dan).

Young women are named by their father's name until they get married, and then they get their husband's name. So when I was growing up, I was "Sim's Lomie," and if I were married to David within the community, I would be named "David Lomie." For some reason the apostrophe and "s" come off the husband's name, as if David becomes a prefix to my own name, rather than me "belonging" to him.

Once in a while it just becomes too unwieldy to use the generations, when the names become something like "Joe's John's Joe." So then the Amish will use a shortcut when that person gets married, and use his wife's name for identification. So he becomes "Ada Joe." And she becomes "Joe Ada."

When someone outside the Amish is referring to coming to visit David and me, they might say they are going to visit the Furlongs. In the Amish community, they would say they are going to visit "Davids." They pluralize the first name of the father of the family to include the whole family.

Differences between Amish
and Mennonites

*T*he Amish and Mennonites share common European Anabaptist roots. The Anabaptists (including the Swiss Brethren) were often persecuted for their religious beliefs, which differed from the state-sponsored Catholic, and later Lutheran and Reformed churches. The difference most espoused by the Anabaptists was their belief that infant baptism was not biblical and therefore not valid—that one needed to understand that Jesus Christ is one's savior for baptism to have meaning. To make such a choice, they claimed, one needed to be an adult. This is how they got their name—Anabaptist means "Rebaptizer." At the time, this was a derogatory name, which the Anabaptists claimed was inaccurate because they weren't rebaptizing at all, since infant baptism was invalid in the first place. However, this is the name they ended up with, and is the one still used today when referring to this religious group.

In the 1690s, a passionate new convert, Jakob Amman, began admonishing his fellow brethren for what he saw as lack of overall discipline. He wanted stricter adherence to the Anabaptist tenets, such as footwashing, shunning, dress, and the attitude towards people who sympathized with the Anabaptists. The followers of the more established group, led by a well-respected leader named Hans Reist, believed these people, too, could achieve salvation, even though they were not actually Anabaptists. They also believed that refusing to include former church members from communion practices was adhering to the practice of shunning. Not Amman—he claimed that nothing short of refusing to eat or drink with them in all social situations would suffice. He took the hard-line approach and began banning church members who did not agree with him. Needless to say, the two groups split. Amman and his followers became the Amish, and the people who stayed with the Hans Reist group became the Mennonites (named after one of the founders of the movement, Menno Simons). The Mennonites were considered to have the more established viewpoint, while Amman was the fervent new convert, wanting to make changes to the status quo.

The Amish and the Mennonites have altered their positions over the last four hundred years. Their worldviews are quite different from one another today. Most Amish want to be left to their lifestyle without intrusion or challenge, and they require their members to follow the church rules and customs without question. Therefore they do not find a need to convert new members into their group, because their retention rate is high. Conversely, the Mennonites place a high value on becoming "born again." The Mennonites send missionaries all over the world to "spread the word of God." The Amish find this off-putting and deem them "mission-minded," especially when the Mennonites are successful in converting members of the Amish church.

The most common outward difference between the Amish and the Mennonites is that most Amish don't own cars, but most Mennonites do—this is complicated by the fact that a few Amish communities allow cars, and a few Mennonite communities (known as horse-and-buggy Mennonites) do not own cars. And then there are the Old Order Amish versus the New Order Amish, and a whole spectrum of Mennonites, from conservative to liberal—the most conservative can hardly be distinguished from the Amish, and the most liberal cannot be distinguished from mainstream Americans by their mode of dress. Also, not all Mennonite groups maintain the dialect, but nearly all the Amish do.

There is another group often mistaken for Amish or Mennonites. The Amish, the Mennonites, and many other Germans settled in various parts of Pennsylvania in the late 1700s and early 1800s. All spoke the same dialect, which is often referred to as Pennsylvania Dutch, though they weren't all

Amish or Mennonite. These people collectively are referred to as "Pennsylvania Germans." Few of the present generation of Pennsylvania Germans who are not Amish or Mennonite speak the dialect, which makes it more likely that those who speak the dialect are either Amish or Conservative Mennonite.

Terms for "Outsiders"

*T*he most common term the Amish use for referring to people who are not part of their community is "English." I can easily imagine where this term came from, at least once they moved to the United States: the outside world spoke English, whereas the Amish spoke a dialect of German.

Another term the Amish often use is *hoch*, which literally means "high." It is puzzling to try to figure out where this term came from. I have only theories, since no one is old enough to remember. The Amish use a term within the community to describe someone who is proud and does not adhere to the Amish ways, often demonstrated by fancier dress or a desire for forbidden things. The word for this prideful attitude is *hochmute*. *Hoch* could be a short form of *hochmute*. A great deal of emphasis is placed on being humble, and perhaps by deeming others as "high," the Amish feel lowlier or more humble.

Another possible source for this term is in the history of our ancestors. They established themselves as expert farmers in Europe, so that dukes and earls often employed them on their estates. In this way, "high" could literally mean "high society."

The third term is "Yankee." I have heard from a researcher of Amish culture that my home community is the only one that uses this term, and the reason this is so is because many of the first settlers in that area were from New England—hence the term Yankee, and the reason for the regional term.

When someone leaves the Amish community, they hardly ever refer to that person as "gone English." Instead they will say that person is *hoch gange* (gone high); or in my home community, they will say someone has "gone Yankee" or she "yanked over." It is as if they believe one cannot become English, but one can become high or Yankee.